This book is a complete guide for those who are thinking of a church wedding. It is packed with practical information on planning the wedding, forms of service, organizing the reception . . .

There are cost-saving ideas and a detailed plan of the order of events— from six months before, to the day itself.

The book also looks at choosing a partner, setting up home, money matters and family planning. Even more important, it considers the basic ingredients for a successful marriage—one that will last.

Getting Married in Church was first produced in 1979 and has remained a bestseller ever since. This new, completely revised edition brings all the material right up to date.

Mary Batchelor is the author and compiler of a number of bestselling titles for adults and children.

GETTING MARRIED IN CHURCH

Mary Batchelor

A LION PAPERBACK

Oxford · Batavia · Sydney

Text copyright © 1979 and 1987 Mary Batchelor
Illustrations © 1979 Ron Ferns and Kathy Wyatt

Published by
Lion Publishing plc
Sandy Lane West, Oxford, England
ISBN 0 7459 1302 4
Albatross Books Pty Ltd
PO Box 320, Sutherland, NSW 2232, Australia
ISBN 0 86760 881 1

First published 1979
Reprinted 1981, 1982, 1983, 1984, 1985
Revised edition 1987
Reprinted 1988, 1989, 1990

British Library Cataloguing in Publication Data

Batchelor, Mary
  Getting married in Church.—Rev. ed.
  1. Marriage—aspects—
  Christianity
  I. Title
  261.8'3581   BT706

  ISBN 0-7459-1302-4

Printed and bound in Great Britain
by Cox & Wyman Ltd, Reading

CONTENTS

Introduction

You've picked up this book to glance at—perhaps because:

- Your wedding date is fixed
- You're engaged—no date chosen as yet
- There's a wedding in your family soon
- You wonder what it's all about

This year, next year, some time . . . someone close to you will be getting married in church. It may be you, or one of your children, or someone in your circle of family and friends who will involve you in the whole complicated affair.

Are you worried about choosing the dress, the flowers, the house? About booking the hotel, the photographer or the cars? Perhaps you aren't sure how to approach the minister of the church of your choice because you've never spoken to him before.

Getting married begins with one big day and this book is written to help with the thousand and one decisions that go to make that day a success. It also explains the meaning of a wedding in church and the promises exchanged during the service.

But a wedding is really about the lifetime of marriage ahead and this book is full of practical advice and discussion points in preparation for a marriage that will last.

Amber light

Marriage is such an important and far-reaching step that every couple needs to think hard before rushing into it. So first we take a cool hard look at the whole business and ask a few questions. Are we really suited? Will it last? How will my life change?

Green light

Once the wedding date is fixed, there are a hundred and one preparations to be made. We give information that will smooth the way for arranging all the practical details. Further ahead there are the problems of deciding where to live, of budgeting the money and setting up a home that is as you like it.

Married in church

If you plan to get married in church you are planning a Christian wedding. How is this different from a civil ceremony? We go through the marriage service to see what it means as well as looking at what Jesus said about marriage.

1. Choosing a Partner

Many people looking at this book will already have decided on the person they are going to marry. How the choice is made varies in different cultures. But in our society, however they have made their choice, all couples hope for a relationship that is based on love. In fact, no longer 'being in love' is often thought a valid reason for ending a marriage.

What is love?
We use the word to cover a whole range of feelings from trivial to profound. We talk of loving cats,

coffee, Victorian architecture, children, parents or God. In the English language the same word has to do service for very different emotional responses. The love that is adequate for a successful marriage must contain the full spectrum of meanings which includes:

Sexual attraction—the aspect of love most emphasized in Western society. Sex is a very important ingredient of married love, but physical passion alone is not enough to sustain the relationship. It is also possible to be sexually attracted to someone you neither like nor admire.

Affection includes liking and fondness but seems an inadequate definition of love in marriage. Affection is often associated with far less demanding relationships. But the bond of sympathy and goodwill that it creates between two people is an excellent buffer for the strains of life together. Affection helps a couple to put up with each other's quirks and foibles with tolerance and humour.

Friendship supposes shared interests and viewpoints or a willingness to share the other's interests. Friendship remains constant when passion fluctuates. It is important to be on the same wavelength and to anticipate with pleasure the prospect of sharing the day's gossip or of talking over an evening out on your way home together.

Respect First impressions can be deceptive and someone who seemed out of this world can turn out to be only too human and full of faults. The closeness of marriage is bound to uncover all kinds of faults and failings and some couples spare no efforts to let the world at large know of them. Married love needs to be realistic without losing basic respect for the partner as a human being. Respect keeps failings private and on the positive side continues to recognize the other's intrinsic worth.

Romance Most girls long for it and many married women still hope for it. Romance is based on the excitement of the differences between man and woman and includes treating the other as still mysterious, unattainable and special—even after years of marriage! It makes marriage more than merely a sensible agreement for living together and enjoying each other's company.

WHAT DO YOU THINK?
. . . about romance

Romance should end ☐ when the honeymoon does ☐ when the children arrive ☐ when you are middle-aged ☐ never

He should ☐ go on giving her red roses on their anniversary ☐ tell her he loves her at least once a day (though not always using the same three words!) ☐ send her Valentines ☐ go on opening doors for her and standing up when she comes into the room

She should ☐ go on dressing to please him ☐ never go to bed in rollers or bedsocks!

. . . about love

1 Is it possible before marriage when passions are running high to discover if you will be good friends in everyday life? If so, how?

2 Is it possible to go on respecting someone whose faults have become all too clear after weeks/months/years of marriage? How?

3 What is the basis of a good marriage? How would you rate the following in importance?

—Same sense of humour
—Understanding each other
—Sharing same goals/ priorities
—Sharing interests
—Wanting to please each other
—Enjoying working together (e.g. decorating/ shopping/travelling)

Another kind of love

This book is about getting married in church, which means a marriage involving God. The Bible describes God as the source of all love. He *is* love. And he is able to give to those who ask for it the kind of love that will make for lasting marriage.

HOW WELL DO YOU KNOW EACH OTHER?

The kind of love which includes respect as well as sexual attraction, affection as well as romantic excitement, is not likely to occur at a first meeting. How a couple first meet, and the kind of situations in which they normally see each other, will make a difference to their perceptions of each other. Did you:

- meet on holiday in Paris?
- live next door from childhood?
- go to the same church?
- work in the same firm?
- meet through membership of the same outdoor activity club?

Ask yourselves the following questions: have you seen enough of each other in different situations to know how each behaves:

- under stress?
- dealing with money?
- off duty?
- in everyday routine?
- in emergencies?
- with older people/ children/those of different social, educational or cultural groups?

Present-day hazards

Expectations of marriage as a partnership that will bring fulfilment on many levels is probably greater today than ever before. But the demands made are greater too. Most couples today:

- have no extended family living close and depend solely on each other for the fulfilment of practical and emotional needs
- move frequently, because of work, and have insufficient time to build up alternative stable friendships
- meet the pressures of two careers/jobs, with sometimes conflicting demands

- bring up a family with little or no 'granny' help and face considerable financial, physical and emotional strains
- mix in a society where acceptance of divorce and adultery makes faithfulness and permanence in marriage hard to maintain.

Personal hazards

Some marriages have additional built-in factors which can add strain and problems unless they are well thought-out and prepared for in advance. The couple may have different cultural/ethnic backgrounds (black marries white, or Easterner marries Westerner), or different religious/denominational background (Roman Catholic marries Protestant). In such marriages parents and family may exert pressures even when the couple themselves have come to terms with the possible problems.

WHAT DO YOU THINK?

1 Do you expect to be all-sufficient to your partner **or** still to rely on parents/same sex friends/church/club for support, companionship and practical help?
2 Do you intend to discuss possible areas of difficulty beforehand, as well as being ready to talk them through together as they crop up?
3 How much notice would you take of parents' prejudices/wishes/feelings?
4 Do you expect to share decision-making between you? If you expect one or other to take the lead, have you talked about which one will fill the role?

WHY GET MARRIED ANYWAY?

Many couples nowadays live together without getting married. They say:

- We love each other enough not to tie each other down.
- What's in a bit of paper anyway?
- Either of us can end the relationship when we wish and no harm done.
- Marriage would make me feel trapped.
- We are better off financially this way.

There is no good answer to the last statement and it is time that tax laws were altered in favour of marriage. But the other arguments for avoiding the full commitment of marriage tend to be half-truths, or imply the selfishness of the speaker. Marriage may seem risky but living together without marriage can create other, greater risks.

- Two people who drift into living together often fail to think through the implications of such a relationship in the way that couples approaching marriage are encouraged to do.
- Every steady sexual relationship creates strong bonds. What the Bible teaches is that living together in this way makes you 'one flesh' in a way that no mutual consent to part can lightly undo. When the bond is broken at least one of the pair is likely to be seriously hurt, whether there is a marriage certificate to prove the point or not. On the practical level, the partners may also lack legal and financial protection.

The marriage ceremony involves more than a 'bit of paper'. It is a public declaration before family and friends of your love and determination to be faithful to each other. From now on they accept and treat you as one unit. It 'registers' your relationship, so that it has legal status and recognition. Within that framework, the relationship has the necessary stability and security to develop and flourish.

2. A Church Wedding

The kind of marriage mentioned so far has been a civil ceremony, recognized by the state. The wedding is conducted at the local Register Office by the Superintendent Registrar of the district. The couple make the required legal statements in the presence of witnesses before signing the register and being furnished with their 'marriage lines' which prove them man and wife in the eyes of the law.

But statistics show that, in Britain anyway, at least half the couples getting married every year are married in church. That ceremony incorporates the civil requirements but implies much more too. A wedding in church brings God into the marriage.

Christians believe that marriage is God's institution, given by him as the best and right way for a permanent, faithful relationship between a man and woman. There are many different reasons why couples do in fact choose to marry in church. Which of the following reasons seem valid to you?

- It's traditional.
- The setting is beautiful.
- The organ music is moving and we like the church bells.
- The ceremony is more solemn and momentous.
- A Register Office wedding is not significant enough.
- Vows made in church count more.
- Our parents want us to marry in church.
- It's more romantic.
- We want to bring God into it.

Here are some actual reasons given by couples for getting married in church:

'I've always wanted a white wedding . . . it's the official joining of Michael and myself, so it is important that it is an occasion to look back on and tell our children about.'

'I'm not deeply religious but I do believe in God and I always wanted to get married in church to have that blessing. Of course the glamour is wonderful but you are also taking a vow and I want that to mean something.'

'I do believe that getting married is to do with

God and what better place to get married than in church?'

'We believe in God and wanted to make our vows in his presence and in the company of our church family—those who share our beliefs.'

'We wanted to be showered with God's blessings and to be guided by him in our future life together—a marriage needs God!'

One bridegroom admitted: 'We wanted to get married in church and our parents wanted it done the traditional way . . . We went into the preparation for marriage with open minds, and after meeting the rector two or three times we began thinking on a much more serious level about the whole of life, not just marriage . . . It has changed our lives, there's no two ways about it, and given us new direction and pleasure.'

PROMISES, PROMISES!

A wedding ceremony conducted in church includes the statements made in a civil ceremony and required by law, but adds much more beside.

For ever!

First—and most surprising, perhaps, at a time when one in three marriages ends in divorce, the couple promise to stay together as husband and wife 'till death us do part, according to God's holy law'. Marriage consecrated in church is marriage for life.

You may think such a promise unrealistic in days when:

- people change—and their requirements for a partner may change too
- couples live longer—so they may face fifty or sixty years together
- divorce is more readily obtained

If you feel that way and consider, in theory at least, that divorce is a reasonable way to end a marriage that has not lived up to expectations, then vows in church are not for you. But, as one vicar remarked, couples *don't* come to the altar thinking that if it doesn't work they'll get a divorce. At the outset everyone determines to make a go of it.

Whatever happens!

Second—both bride and groom promise to stand by each other whatever circumstances may arise. 'For better, for worse, for richer, for poorer, in sickness and in health.' They may face unemployment or early retirement, accident or incurable illness, the birth of a disabled child or the care of elderly parents—but each will stick by the other. Of course there are plenty of good times in most people's lives and they will enjoy together the 'better, richer, health' side of the bargain too.

No one else in your life

Third—in church both promise that 'forsaking all other' they will be 'faithful' to each other for the whole of their lives. Some couples begin their marriage with the tacit or spoken agreement that either is free to take a lover from time to time. Some marriage counsellors advise an 'affair' to freshen up a tired marriage.

People who think that way cannot honestly make vows in church, where they promise no adultery. The church did not think up this restriction to make life harder, nor is it a leftover relic of a less tolerant age. The Bible model of marriage—which is God's original model—includes absolute faithfulness on the part of both husband and wife. Licence to commit adultery underrates the importance of the sexual bond in marriage. That does not mean that Christian marriage involves a harsh and unforgiving attitude on the part of one partner toward the other, if either one breaks this or any other vow. A Christian partner should combine high personal standards of faithfulness with understanding and forgiveness towards the other—impossible without the outside help from God which being a Christian implies!

Bringing God into marriage

Last—but most important of all—marriage in church brings God into the two lives that are becoming one. The ceremony is not a legal contract but takes place in the context of a church service, with God as chief witness to the proceedings. God does not want to leave those who make demanding promises like these simply to their own devices. He is not only present at the wedding ceremony but is also willing to be concerned in the working out of the marriage in the days and years that will follow, bringing his help and strength and forgiveness to those couples who ask for it. When Jesus was on earth he was guest at a wedding and brought happiness and joy to the couple when he turned water into wine. That miracle is symbolic of the way in which Jesus can still bring fresh life and renewed joy into any marriage to which he is invited today.

WHAT WILL IT COST IN POUNDS AND PENCE?

Most people who get married in church want the package deal, which will include what some refer to—as if talking of Christmas dinner—as 'all the trimmings'. It is assumed that a church wedding will involve the couple and their families in special outfits, smart cars, an expensive wedding breakfast and far more. But the actual cost of a church wedding service is almost exactly the same as a Register Office wedding, allowing for the fact that the fee for marriage includes payment for use of the building, whereas the rates go to pay for the use of the Register Office.

If a couple choose a church wedding because they want a Christian wedding service, they can still keep it simple and inexpensive. But it is more often the case that a couple start off by wanting a traditional and glamorous wedding and feel that a church wedding is the only possible setting for it.

It is a pity that the two kinds of wedding have become identified with two such different styles of getting married. Register offices are by no means the dingy, dark places they once were. The registrar conducts the service in a sympathetic and dignified way and there are flowers and music, as well as provision for taking photographs. But the setting is still far from most brides' dreams of a white wedding.

The impression (soon verified by price quotations) that a church wedding will be very expensive is reinforced by a glance through the magazines produced for brides. The advertisements imply that every bride expects to wear a fabulously expensive wedding gown, enjoy a large reception and be treated to glossy photographs, exotic flowers, and an out-of-this-world honeymoon, before returning to a brand-new fully-furnished home of her own.

WHAT DO YOU THINK?

1 Do you think that weddings, like many other things in life, have become too commercialized?

2 Are any of the following important to you, as a way of showing what your marriage means—or would you choose them just to follow a pattern or to please parents?

- special wedding clothes
- luxury wedding cars
- special honeymoon
- expensive wedding reception
- professional photographs/video
- professional flower arrangements

3. Preparing for Marriage

Once the wedding is arranged, all the available time seems to be taken up with preparations for the actual day. One bride summed it up for them all when she said, 'I want everything to go perfectly.' Of course everything must be right on the day and that will involve meticulous planning.

But the day will come and go whereas the marriage will last for ever. Or will it? The number of marriage breakdowns is not reassuring. Not just the ceremony, but marriage itself requires planning beforehand if it is to go smoothly when the time

comes. It is even more important to find time to do this planning together than to put all available energy into the wedding day itself.

THE LUCK OF THE DRAW?

Many people speak of marriage as if it were a lottery. You pick either a winner or a loser. That kind of approach makes planning and preparation for marriage a waste of time. But although no one can guarantee that nothing will go wrong (and the same is true for the best planned wedding day), it *is* possible to smooth out beforehand some of the areas that could cause trouble and difficulty if they had never been anticipated or talked through before marriage.

Know yourself

If you are going to be mature enough to cope with the relationship of marriage you need to have some idea of your own strengths and weaknesses. How well do you know yourself? Try answering these alternatives:

Easy

- Am I at my best in the morning **or** late in the evening?
- Do I like to eat little and often **or** 'stoke up well' at longer intervals?
- Am I good at spending money **or** better at saving it?
- Do I like staying at home **or** prefer to go out and about?

- Am I shy in company **or** good with a crowd of people?
- Am I always punctual **or** content to get there in the end?
- Do I like working **or** blossom on holiday or at leisure?
- Am I ambitious/ competitive **or** content to tick over and be happy?

More difficult

- Do I throw temper tantrums when annoyed **or** sulk/get my own back in words that wound?
- Do I nurse long-term grudges **or** find it easy to forgive and forget?
- Am I tolerant towards those who think differently **or** do I judge others harshly?
- Do I like making decisions **or** prefer to follow another's lead?
- Am I painstaking/ perfectionist **or** easy-going, able to dash things off?
- Am I often tense and uptight **or** laid back and relaxed?

Hard

- Can I laugh at myself?
- Do I find it hard to say sorry?
- Do I like my own way— and how do I react when I don't get it?
- Can I enter into others' feelings and experiences?
- Do I expect to be a helper—or to be helped, or both, at different times?
- Can I admit when I'm wrong?
- Do I need a good deal of reassuring and ego-boosting?

Know your partner

When you have answered these questions as honestly as you can, ask them again about your partner. If you don't know many of the answers, perhaps you haven't yet discovered enough about the person you are going to live with. You won't find out everything in advance, but it's common sense to have some idea of what makes your husband/wife-to-be tick.

Most important of all, perhaps, take time to go over both sets of questions and answers together. Learn more about yourself and each other by comparing notes on your own assessments and your partner's. A little gentle but firm exploring and defining of each other's strengths and weaknesses is valuable preparation for the sharing of married life.

IN THE BACKGROUND

Everyone comes to marriage with a past. Everything that has happened to you since you were a young child—and before that—has made you the kind of person you now are. Your upbringing, your parents' relationship to each other as well as to you, the number of brothers and sisters you have—all these and a hundred other factors have gone into making you *you*.

Parental attitudes

There are a hundred and one different patterns of family life. You may have been:

• constantly praised and applauded	**or**	criticized and belittled
• the centre of attention and anxious care	**or**	largely left to your own devices

● disciplined strictly	**or**	given your own way
● pressured to achieve at school/college	**or**	prevented from achieving your full potential
● taken to church/ Sunday school	**or**	had no religious instruction

You may have had:

● happily married parents	**or**	been involved in stormy scenes and marriage break-up
● no father	**or**	two (one step-father)
● a typical middle-class home	**or**	belonged to a cultural/ ethnic minority

Priorities

Family values vary enormously. Top priorities in your home may have been:

- ● Money
- ● Education
- ● Careers
- ● Home and furnishings
- ● Church-going
- ● Food
- ● Health
- ● Social life
- ● Books
- ● Hobbies
- ● Status symbols

You may have clung to parental values or reacted violently against them. You may have been unaware of them or have carefully thought through the issues involved and come to your own opinion about their wisdom or rightness.

You may have happy memories of childhood or be handicapped by such painful memories that you have banished them to the furthest recesses of your mind. But memories don't go away. Unhealed wounds need careful and gentle attention. Left to fester they will harm your future relationships and the new family you will both be creating.

Now, within the warmth and security of your shared love, you can afford to be honest with yourself and each other, and find healing for the hurts and wrongs of childhood. It may be the first time that you have got the past into true perspective as an adult. Grudges and resentments may need to be shed and forgiveness received and given.

When you plan a marriage in church you are asking God into your new relationship. When you open up the past to him as well as to each other he is able to forgive, to help *you* to forgive, and to heal the past. He can even use those painful experiences to enrich and strengthen your future lives together.

PREPARING FOR SEX

The facts of life today:

- Only about one bride in six is a virgin
- Casual sex ('no strings attached') has become fairly commonplace from teen years on
- Living together without getting married—and keeping the options open—has become acceptable to many
- Sex is commonly an accepted part of 'going steady' or engagement

(It remains to be seen how far new understandings about health will cause a swing in thinking. It is now recognized that some serious diseases are largely spread by sexual contact—also that girls who have

had a number of sexual partners since their teens
are more prone to certain forms of cancer.)

The Bible takes a different view of sex. The
early Christians lived for the most part in societies
where attitudes toward sex were similar to those of
our own day, but Jesus and the apostles still
maintained that:

● the sex act makes two people one—that is, it creates a unique and deep pair bond

● we are more than a high form of animal life—the physical act of sex involves a sharing of the whole personality

● a sexual relationship is only appropriate and right within the context of a permanent and totally committed relationship— i.e. marriage

● sex in marriage involves joyful self-giving, not self-gratification

● sex should be an important and continuing part of the marriage relationship

(The Bible references which form the basis of these
statements can be found in the New Testament:
Mark's Gospel chapter 10, verses 6–9; and the first
letter to the Corinthians, chapter 6, verse 1 and
chapter 7, verse 5.)

Sex is meant to be part of a whole, complete and
lasting relationship between one man and one
woman. Many people treat sex as a bit of fun with
no strings attached. But the strings are there and
one partner or the other is likely to be badly hurt
because sex has been used in a way it was never
intended to be. Sex for kicks has a habit of aiming
hard kicks at those who misuse it—either at the time
or in the forming of further relationships. If it is to
be enjoyed in its true context sex must be part of a
total sharing—the night's sleep, the day's chores,
the pleasures, worries, decisions and experiences of

two lives joined together in a fully committed relationship.

The gap between what the Bible teaches and what our own society approves is obvious. Not much has been done about helping people to recognize the practical value of Bible standards towards healthy, happy sex or in giving young couples positive guidance to carry them out. At present, all too often, older churchgoers close their eyes to what is *actually* happening, and young Christian couples assent outwardly to Bible teaching but experience a full sexual relationship before marriage just the same—often with feelings of guilt. Young people who intend keeping to Bible standards look in vain for more positive help about the right way to handle sex in their own relationships. Non-churchgoers see the Bible stance as unrealistic or even positively harmful.

Answers to some questions

Q. Isn't it a bit old-fashioned of the church to say that you shouldn't have sex before marriage?

A. Easy sex and adultery are old-fashioned too, come to that. But, agreed, the Christian view is different from, and more difficult than, popular ideas. But there are still many young people who feel pressured into having sex when they instinctively want to keep themselves for the person they marry. The church sees sex as such a special way for a man and woman to give themselves to each other and express their oneness that it properly fits only the special context of marriage. Sex has its fullest meaning only within a settled, lasting relationship where everything else is shared too.

Taken out of this setting, sex can bring pain, frustration and exploitation to one or other partner. Caring, sharing and making a home and family together are the proper accompaniments of the sex relationship.

Q. We're engaged now, so isn't it all right to have sex?

A. A lot of people who would not go to bed with any boy or girl friend feel that being engaged makes it different. We're getting married anyway, runs the argument, so why wait? But even engagement is not the same as living together and sharing all the experiences of life in a relationship that has been publicly declared and pledged. While it is right that the physical relationship should gradually deepen—along with a fuller understanding of each other at every level—during engagement, the complete giving to each other in the sex act still rightly belongs to marriage. A short engagement reduces the strains.

Q. How can we be sure that we shall be suited if we don't make love before we get married?

A. Furtive love-making in the back of a car, or while parents are out, is not a very good test of whether you will be able to respond to each other. A quick peck on the cheek is not the only alternative to full sex before marriage. Obviously you will discover during courtship and deepening intimacy, if you find each other physically attractive, or if either of you seems 'cold'. Provided you are both looking forward to making love fully there need be no worries.

Q. Won't clamping down on sex now make for problems when the honeymoon arrives?

A. Some people certainly imply that keeping sex for

marriage is going to impose unhealthy strains that will make it impossible to 'let go' and enjoy sex when the time comes. That just is not true in practice, unless one or both already has some kind of hang-up about sex. When you both agree to practise self-control until you are married this does not mean that you are harmfully repressing your sexual instincts. False feelings of guilt about sex, or some unhappy experience in the past *could* cause problems and both partners need to talk through such difficulties and get professional help beforehand when necessary.

Q. How important is sex in marriage?

A. Very important. The sex relationship can be an indicator of the health of the marriage—rather like taking your temperature to see if it's normal. Of course there can be difficulties which need a doctor's treatment or outside advice, but on the whole, where there is a loving and trusting relationship, then the physical love-making is likely to be satisfying. On the other hand, where there is argument, bitterness, jealousy or resentment, these things are likely to hinder and spoil a couple's sex life.

Making love can express passion, tenderness, affection and a oneness that is much more than the oneness of body. It can also be fun! When husband and wife feel especially close, or after they have quarrelled and made it up, making love can be the perfect way to tell each other how they feel. Being satisfied does not depend solely on getting the technique right. What matters most to husband and wife is showing their love and if it doesn't work quite perfectly for both one time, there is always another time. If either partner continues to have difficulty in making love, then it is best to get advice either from your doctor or from one of the counselling organizations.

Should I tell all?

Most couples come to marriage eager to share everything. Being in love makes each want to tell all. It is good to talk together of childhood memories, hopes and fears. But some have had past sexual experiences which they may now regret and which may leave them with feelings of guilt. It may be important to make someone a confidante, but should that person be the one you are going to marry? Take into account that:

- every couple is different—in temperament, background and circumstances
- some facts (e.g. an abortion, illegitimate child) may become known later on anyway
- other people—innocently or with malice aforethought—might 'tell'
- some 'confessions' bring relief to the one who tells but pain and lasting distress to the hearer

---

WHAT DO YOU THINK?

Should a husband or wife-to-be:

1 . . . keep the past a closed book as far as sexual experiences are concerned?

2 . . . indicate that there have been past experiences but in a general way, not giving names or details?

3 . . . tell all—in detail—so that the memories are now shared by both?

4 . . . be honest about any facts that might otherwise come to light at a later stage and in a more hurtful way?

5 . . . discuss together which way to tackle the problem, aiming to be loving (considering the other's good) and as honest as you both can cope with?

LOOKING AHEAD

You are much more likely to spend time talking about your future together than your separate pasts. There are some areas where discussion beforehand can prevent possible friction in the early days of marriage. For example:

Money

One person's extravagance may be another's lifeline. Tick those things on the list which seem important to you and see if your partner agrees:

☐ Meals out   ☐ Books
☐ Long telephone calls   ☐ Exotic holidays
☐ Car   ☐ Stereo equipment
☐ Pets   ☐ Clothes

Do you prefer to buy now, pay later, *or* to pay on the nail (wait to afford it)? Have you decided:

- which one will mainly handle finance?
- who will pay for what—when both are working?
- whether to have a joint bank account?

Roles

Will you share out the chores (washing/ironing/cleaning/shopping/decorating, etc.) according to:

- who leaves home last/arrives home first/has more time off?
- age-old sex stereotypes?
- skills and preferences?

Home

Do you want your home to be mainly:

- a place for you both to relax in?
- somewhere to entertain your family and friends?
- a place that will look good and do you credit?

Leisure

If you met because both are fanatical cyclists or bell-ringers, you will have the same ideas on leisure activities. If not, have you decided:

- how much time he should have out with the boys, or she with the girls?
- whether she is expected to support his local football matches/cricket team, and he her ambitions to run a marathon?
- if each will give the other freedom to go to judo/weightlifting/keep fit alone?
- how much leisure time you will plan to spend together?

Parents

Talk through your attitudes to both sets of parents/families. How responsible will you feel, given the particular circumstances, to visit, entertain or support them?

Children

Do you both want children? If not, can you sort out your differences? If you do, at what stage would you plan to start a family? How will you expect to care for them (fulltime parent *or* shared responsibility *or* nursery/child minder/nanny *or* obliging granny—check with her first!)?

Church and faith

If you go to churches of different denominations, now is the time to sort out what you plan to do about it once you are married. Differences like this can be overcome provided you both have in common a genuine faith in Christ and determination to follow him.

The New Testament teaches that it is impossible for a Christian to join in any very close partnership with someone who does not share his or her faith. Being a committed Christian means putting Jesus first—even before husband or wife. No partner is going to stand for anyone else coming first unless he or she has the same priority. But when both put loyalty to Jesus first, they discover that their love and loyalty to each other is increased, not diminished.

4. Countdown to the Day

Engagements tend to be far less formal these days but spreading the news that a marriage has been arranged gives family and friends—as well as the couple themselves—a chance to prepare for the

event. Some couples like to keep to the traditional pattern according to which:

- the prospective bridegroom asks permission of her father to marry the girl of his choice (these days this is almost always a matter of courtesy, to give her parents the news first!)

- he buys an engagement ring (or they choose it together)
- both tell close relatives and friends (going together to see as many as possible)
- parents put an announcement in the local/national newspapers

If you decide to dispense with all these rituals, remember to keep family relationships sweet by making sure that both sets of parents have the news first and that aunts, great aunts and so on get the news from source!

PREPARATIONS FOR THE DAY

Planning can begin as much as a year before the wedding day and it is a help to work out your own timetable for booking and ordering all that is needed. Certain things must be arranged well in advance but will need to be confirmed nearer the date for your peace of mind.

It is fatal to set a definite shopping expedition for the various wedding outfits—they so often end up as wasted journeys—but begin looking round for a good while beforehand and don't leave the foot-slogging job of matching accessories to the last few weeks!

Carry round a sample of any colours to be matched whenever you may be near shops! If you can't use a piece of the actual material, try using the colour charts provided by decorating shops for matchmaker type paints. These provide literally hundreds of shades and I have always found one that is an exact match for any material I've been using. Just carry the card, with the correct shade marked, for instant reference.

If you have set your heart on getting married on a particular Saturday in summer you may need to begin planning more than a year ahead. But it is best not to bank on a day until you have seen the minister of the church of your choice. Ring him first to arrange the day and time before embarking on any other bookings.

The countdown that follows gives some idea of timing. More details on each topic follow:

Twelve months (or more) before

- Contact minister/priest and arrange date and time
- Book hotel or book hire of marquee (September is the most popular month for hire)

Six months before

- Book hall (for reception) and caterers
- Plan menu (if catering yourself) and order in which to make and freeze dishes
- Compile guest list (hotel/caterer requires approximate number only at this stage)
- Choose best man, bridesmaids, ushers, etc.
- Book honeymoon
- Book florist
- Begin looking at dresses (or patterns/material) for bride's and bridesmaids' dresses

Five months before

● Book wedding car(s) (and check if help is available from car-owning friends to top up transport requirements)
● Book photographer and/or video equipment/ operator
● Plan wedding present list—register with store to handle it if required

Four months before

● Order wedding stationery
● Order wedding cake
● Discuss menus with hotel/caterer (unless agreed at first booking)

Three months before

● Make cake (if homemade)—it needs at least three months to mature
● Confirm with minister about form of service/bell-ringing/choir, etc.
● Choose hymns and form of service for printed sheet
● Visit doctor or Family Planning Clinic
● Finalize honeymoon arrangements when necessary
● See Registrar (if needed at non-Anglican service), or arrange calling of banns (Church of England)
● Choose wedding ring(s)
● Book overnight accommodation when needed for night before for bridegroom/guests

Two months before

● Send out invitations (strictly speaking, these should go out six weeks beforehand but more notice is often needed, especially for a summer wedding)
● Plan music with organist/choir
● Arrange passport change of name for bride if required

- Have inoculations if needed for honeymoon abroad
- List replies to invitations
- List gifts received and write prompt letters of thanks
- Buy gifts for bridesmaids, etc.
- Shop for additional holiday clothes (if not already bought)
- Complete form supplied for newspaper announcement

Six weeks before

- Give more information to florist (sketch of dress, sample of material)

Four weeks before

- Keep up to date with guest list and 'thank you' letters for gifts
- Arrange for hire clothes for bridegroom, etc. when necessary
- See hairdresser and have perm (if customary)— take headdress/hat to show him/her
- Book hair appointment for wedding day
- Arrange seating plan for reception

Three weeks to two weeks before

- Put almond paste on cake (allow two weeks to dry out before icing is applied)
- Arrange hire of cake stand and knife (unless hotel/baker is providing them)
- Confirm details with photographer/car firm/ florist and other firms involved
- Check journey time to church, allowing for traffic hold-ups, Saturday traffic, etc.

Ten days before

- Collect tickets and travel documents from travel agents

Seven days to one day before

- Ice cake—five days needed for all the coats to dry
- Finalize seating plan—write place names (unless ordered)
- Bride try on full wedding outfit—including underwear—break in shoes at home if necessary
- Pack honeymoon luggage and check arrangements to take luggage and going-away outfits to hotel
- Return form for newspaper announcement(s)
- Check that best man has service sheets
- Have full rehearsal in church

That countdown tells its own story of the bewildering number of arrangements and bookings to be made in the coming months. So:

- make plenty of check lists of your own and tick off items as you go
- make bookings well in advance—this way you get what you really want and save yourself hassle
- keep a running list of names and phone numbers of firms concerned for future contacts and confirmations

But before you arrive at the stage of making firm bookings, you will want to do some shopping around, so as to choose exactly what you want and to pay the most reasonable prices. If you haven't the time to enquire into every separate item you may prefer to make a booking with a firm that caters for every aspect of the wedding, fixing you up with cars, florist, photographer and all. Here are some guidelines:

- Consult the yellow pages telephone directory (under Weddings—or separate topics—florists, stationers, etc.)

- Pick the brains of friends who have organized a wedding and whose judgement you can trust
- Get several estimates—at least three—and compare value for money
- Don't be rushed into any decisions whatever pressure is put on you—you can always phone back later that same day—so give yourself a breathing space
- Don't be tempted to spend more than you can afford or feel comfortable about
- Don't try to compete with other people's weddings—it's the quality of the marriage, not the glamour of the wedding, that really counts
- Always check if VAT is included in estimates (and service, where a hotel or restaurant is concerned)

WHAT WILL IT COST— AND WHO PAYS?

Specialist magazines give alarming totals for the cost of wedding, honeymoon and setting up home and a glance at the advertisements they carry may confirm your worst fears. Some firms report that a growing number of couples are accepting payment for flowers, photographs, etc. in lieu of wedding presents from relatives. But for couples whose conscience as well as whose purse dictates a limit to outgoings on the day, there are plenty of ways of cutting costs without spoiling the wedding.

At one time there were firmly-fixed rules about who paid for what at a wedding. Things are much more flexible now but it's as well to know the rules, whether you decide to stick to them or not.

In theory . . .

The bride's parents pay for:
- bride's and bridesmaids' wedding clothes
- reception
- flowers for church and reception
- cars
- photographs
- wedding cake plus boxes and postage
- invitations and service sheets

The bridegroom pays for:
- licence, banns and certificate
- all church service expenses
- bouquets for bride and attendants
- flower-sprays for both mothers
- buttonholes for himself and best man
- wedding ring
- gifts for bridesmaids and best man
- honeymoon

In practice

The cost of the reception may be shared by both sets of parents—though it is up to the groom's family to suggest this—or it may be met by bride and groom if they can afford it more easily! The bride will probably buy her own wedding dress and the bridesmaids may be happy to pay for theirs. If they do, they should naturally have a big say in what they wear—they are sure to choose something that they can use for parties afterwards. A bit of tact is needed to sort this one out. As for the honeymoon, the bride may chip in as she would for any holiday.

5. Getting Down to Business

We have looked at the overall plan. Now it's time to check through item by item.

The wedding breakfast
This is probably the most expensive part of the wedding. Begin by drawing up an approximate guest list, remembering that bride and groom usually invite roughly the same number of people. It's only courteous to consult both sets of parents, especially if one (or both) is footing the bill. Don't forget an invitation to the minister and his wife, or

the priest. Try to include those who have known and cared about you since childhood, even though they may be less interesting than more recent, younger friends.

After the first shock at the total, you will probably pare down the list several times. Where money is no problem, you can go straight ahead with enquiries, remembering that for a guest list of one hundred or more you need to book earlier, as fewer hotels can accommodate such numbers. Most families will have to choose between a less expensive menu/cheaper hotel and cutting numbers drastically.

Invitations

The bride's parents are normally host and hostess and their names top the invitations as a rule. If the couple themselves plan to give the wedding, their two names appear instead. If parents are divorced, the names of those hosting the wedding should be used, whether natural parents or parent plus step-parent. It is often helpful for non-local guests if you include a map with the invitation, showing the location of church and reception.

Hotels

Arrange to see the banqueting manager and have a list of queries ready. Some hotels, especially those that are part of a national chain, may offer a very good deal which will include *free*, such extras as:

- use of bedrooms where guests can change and freshen up

- rooms for the bridal couple to change in before going away

- table trimmings to match bride's colour scheme
- cake stand and knife
- services of a toastmaster to assist as MC

- free overnight accommodation for bride and groom at any of their hotels
- reduced charges for overnight accommodation for guests

Hotels will suggest a number of different menus at fixed prices per head. These range from finger buffets to a sumptuous buffet meal. Here are two samples, from least expensive to middle of the range, taken from the weddings brochure of a national chain of hotels:

Inexpensive
Assorted sandwiches
sausage rolls
spicy chicken pieces
cheese and pineapple sticks
cocktail sausages
crisps and cheeselets

Mid-range
Egg mayonnaise
ham and pineapple rolls
deep fried chicken
goujons of plaice
baked jacket potatoes
mixed seasonal salad
strawberry gateau
and cream
coffee

They will probably offer a package deal for drinks too.

Restaurant, Cafe or 'Pub'
These may be cheaper than an hotel. Check on facilities for couple to change.

Hall
You may know of a suitable school or village hall for hire, or you can contact your local council for their list of available halls. Friends can often help to make

a bare, unattractive room look cheerful and festive. Check on cloakroom facilities. Bride and groom would probably have to return home to change.

Caterers

Plenty of good cooks have set up as caterers and advertise in the local free press. Most will offer fixed price menus varying from finger buffet to full meal. Check if they:

- provide crockery/cutlery
- serve food/drink
- clear and wash up afterwards

Personal recommendation is important when choosing a caterer, or you could try out their services for a small party first.

Marquee

A lovely marquee in the garden can be idyllic. It can also be expensive. But remember that cost of hire is likely to include lining, tables, tablecloths, cutlery, chandelier, crockery and chairs (price may vary according to type of chair provided).

DIY catering

This is not an impossible task with the aid of freezers to spread the timing of the work and the right kind of friends to see to last-minute preparation and presentation. Women's magazines and some cookery books offer suggested menus for large numbers and give advice on the order in which to make and freeze batches. Careful planning is the keynote.

> ### Cost Saver
> Reduce numbers for the reception and follow up with an informal party at parents' home with food you have prepared yourself.

Photographs

Good photographs are important. With tapes and videos they form the only lasting record of the day. Personal recommendation from friends and a good batch of professional wedding photos to prove the case are probably the best guides to choice.

Beware of firms that:

- insist on a minimum order
- offer expensive packaging (albums, etc.)
- operate as national companies—they often employ local amateurs for wedding photography

Beware too of the well-qualified photographer (with letters after his/her name!) who may send a part-timer to photograph your wedding.

Video film may be shot by a professional or equipment may be hired for a friend with know-how to film for you. Remember that the minister's permission must be asked before filming in church.

> ### Cost Saver
> Don't economize by having an inferior photographer who is cheaper. Instead engage a first-class firm but order fewer photographs to be taken. Use skilled amateurs among your guests for back-up (ask them beforehand and pay for film/processing).

The cake

Look out for a good local baker/confectioner whose cakes you have sampled. (Some make small sample size fruit cakes for sale, using same mixture.)

If you are making your own cake, it is worth making an extra, separate cake which can be taken straight to the kitchen and cut up in advance to save waiting for the cake-cutting ceremony.

Cake knife and stand may be:

- provided free by hotel
- provided by baker who makes cake—with returnable large deposit to cover risk of theft
- provided by baker at hire charge plus deposit

Cost Savers

- Have single or two-tier cake or three-tier in smaller sizes
- Make your own. Someone in one of the two families might be proud to make the cakes and there should be time to go to icing classes and learn how to complete the work of art. There are mail firms that supply pillars, decorations.
- Fresh flowers to match the bride's bouquet are sometimes placed on top of the cake.

NB Some bakers will do an almond and royal icing service for your home-made cake but this can work out very expensive.

Flowers

Choose a florist whose judgement you trust or whose creativeness you admire and whose finished work you have seen. Some have an album of brides and bouquets to help you choose. A good florist will take into account the height and colouring of the bride, as well as the colours and textures of materials to be used for the dresses. Tell her/him before the day if you wish to have the bouquet pressed afterwards, as flowers must be dry. She/he will then avoid spraying it before delivery to keep it fresh.

Cost Saver

See to church flowers and table decorations at the reception yourselves. Check that there are no seasonal restrictions on flowers or colours at church and that the official flower arranger is happy to give you a free hand. She and her helpers might even be willing to decorate the church to your specifications.

Wedding Dress

The sky is the limit as far as cost is concerned. In deciding the level, remember the additional cost if bridegroom and other leading men need morning dress to complement bride's outfit.

Cost Savers

Buy second-hand, or borrow; make your own from scratch, or buy a cut-out and ready-to-sew dress; or hire.

Stationery

Look for a printer who will print what *you* want. Only accept package orders if they are good value and what you really require. There are endless offers of printed paraphernalia. 'Handcrafted personalized place-cards' and 'personalized wedding car ribbons' are a must *only* if they are just what you have always hankered for.

Cars
Remember, if you want something special (vintage car or white Rolls-Royce), you need to be extra prompt with booking.

Cost Saver
Order one car only from the hire firm. This will make two trips to the church, first taking the bride's mother and bridesmaids, then returning for the bride and her father. After the service it will take bride and groom to the reception. Arrange with members of the family and willing friends to take the rest of the guests from church to reception. Organize well in advance and give those offering lifts a written note of the guests they are to transport. Best man/ushers should have full list. No guest should be left feeling stranded!

WEDDING PRESENTS

Draw up your own personal list with the aid of the one given. If you decide to make use of a store that offers a wedding gift service, you will be taken round the departments, and the design, size and make of the items you require will be noted. Guests can phone or call at the store to order their gift which will be wrapped and delivered to you with a note of the giver.

If you prefer to keep things less commercial and deal direct with guests and friends a good method is to buy a number of very small pads with perforated pages. Write a different gift on each page, noting all necessary details, and mixing large presents with inexpensive ones in each book. Friends who inquire can be given a book from which they tear out the page with the gift of their choice. This scheme avoids duplicating gifts and saves waiting for the original gift list to be returned and checked before being sent to the next person.

Remember to keep a list of gifts received, alongside your guest-reply list, and tick as soon as you have written a letter of thanks. Keep up to date!

Suggestions for your wedding list

KITCHEN
baking tins
bread bin
bread board and
 knife
can opener
carving dish
casserole dishes
cheese grater
chopping board
coffee grinder
coffee maker
colander
cookery books
corkscrew
dishwasher
electric carver
electric kettle/jug
food processor/
 mixer
freezer
frying pan
garlic press
grapefruit knife
iron

ironing board
kitchen knives
lemon squeezer
measuring jugs
microwave oven
mixing bowls
mugs
oven-to-table ware
pedal bin
pressure cooker
refrigerator
rolling pin
salad bowl/servers
sandwich toaster
saucepans
scales
scissors
sieve
slow cooker
spice rack
tea towels
toaster
trays
vegetable rack
washing machine

washing up bowl,
 etc.
wok
wooden spoons
yogurt maker

DINING ROOM
butter dish
cake dish
cake knife
candlesticks
canteen of cutlery
 (or separate
 items for set)
carving set
cheeseboard/knife
coffee set
decanter
dinner/tea service
 (best and
 everyday)
egg cups
fruit dishes/
 spoons

grapefruit spoons
hostess trolley/
     tray (heated)
pastry forks
pastry slice
place mats
ramekin dishes
sauce boat
soda syphon/
     stream
steak knives
tablecloths/
     napkins
teapot
toast rack
trolley
     (lightweight)
water jug/
     glasses
wine glasses
     (various)

BATHROOM
bath mat
bathroom cabinet
bathroom scales

**CLEANING
CUPBOARD**
brooms and
     brushes
carpet shampooer
dusters
dustpan and brush
floor mop/sponge
vacuum cleaner

BEDROOM
blankets
duvet and covers
electric blanket
pillows
pillow cases

sheets
tea/coffee maker

MISCELLANEOUS
clocks
coffee table
cushions
door mat
flower containers
garden tools
garden furniture
lawn mower
mirrors
plant pot holders
radio
standard lamp
step ladders
table lamp
television set
waste paper
     baskets

6. Planning a Family

Our great-grandmothers took it for granted that babies would arrive with relentless regularity, whether 'planned' or not. After all, in their day, child-bearing was one of the chief results—and purposes—of marriage. Family planning was often frowned upon and rarely reliable. Many babies died at birth or in infancy: it was necessary to have enough for some to survive. And children were a source of income in later years—an investment for old age, when there was no prospect of a state pension.

Today, couples are likely to put forward reasons for *not* having children. A family involves enormous

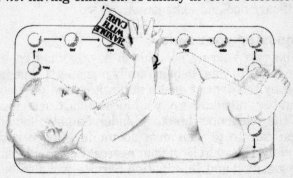

expense—from cradle to higher education. It means loss of earnings for one parent—or the expense of engaging a child-carer.

A family may be a hindrance to strong career ambitions, particularly those of the mother.

Added to such matters of self-concern, many couples fear to bring children into a world threatened by pollution, violence and nuclear war.

Fortunately for the future of the race, there are still many who want to have a family and who see parenthood as a worthwhile and important role in spite of the low status accorded to motherhood in particular and the personal sacrifices involved. In addition, those with a Christian faith believe that the future is under God's control, however threatening the outlook may be.

Couples who decide to have a baby do need to be realistic about what it will cost in terms of money and infringement of personal liberty! Imagining the baby as an unresisting doll, to be dressed prettily and played with, is no preparation for the real thing. No one can really envisage the change of lifestyle that children will bring. Fortunately their presence brings a great deal of fun and happiness as well as self-sacrifice and exhaustion.

Choosing your time

Whatever your decision about having children, you are likely to want help in family planning. Clinics are run by the district health authorities and the phone number and address of your local clinic can be found in the telephone directory under Family Planning. You can go to your own doctor for advice if you prefer. The address of your nearest Family Planning Association and Information Service will also be in

WHAT DO YOU THINK?

1 Should children be the normal follow-on to marriage, special circumstances apart?

2 Is it better to wait until money is freer and the wife's career established before having a baby, or to have the family while you are both young?

3 Is it unfair to have an only child who will be in a minority against two parents?

4 How should parental responsibilities be shared out?

5 Should a wife return to work after maternity leave? If so, what arrangements are best for the baby?

6 Should being a full-time parent at home have higher status in our society? How could that be achieved?

7 What factors will you take into account when deciding whether or not to have a family?

the phone book. These centres provide a consumer service dealing with queries and they publish helpful literature. Their booklet called *Introduction to Family Planning* is available by post.

Two to three months before your wedding, visit the clinic, together if possible. Don't be afraid to discuss your personal feelings and preferences honestly with the doctor who sees you.

Roman Catholic couples will prefer to consult the Catholic Marriage Advisory Council who have eighty regional centres where they provide instruction in the natural method of contraception. Other couples who for ecological reasons prefer natural birth control can go to these centres too.

The following table lists the currently available methods of contraception. Other methods soon to come on the market are the vaginal contraceptive ring and hormonal implants.

Methods of birth control

Method	Who for?	Medical advice needed?	How reliable?	Comments
Combined pill	Her	Yes	Almost 100%	Not suitable for all women
Mini pill	Her	Yes	98%	Not suitable for all women
Injectable	Her	Yes	Almost 100%	Short or long term but for use in special cases only
Intra-uterine Device (IUD or Coil)	Her	Yes	96–98%	Fitted then checked annually: thought to work through preventing egg's growth, so some couples object to using it on moral grounds
Condom (Sheath)	Him	No	97% with careful use	Can be bought at chemist or on prescription
Spermicides		No	Not effective used alone	
Diaphragm (Cap) + Spermicide	Her	Yes	97% with careful use	Right size chosen by doctor. Woman inserts in vagina before intercourse
Sponge + Spermicide	Her	No	85% or less	Used similarly to cap but disposable
Safe Period Methods		Help from trained counsellor	85–93% with careful use	Effectiveness varies with each couple
Sterilization Vasectomy	Her Him	Yes	Occasional failures	Permanent and almost always irreversible so much care/counselling needed before making decision

WHAT DO YOU THINK?

1 Do children hold a marriage together?

2 How would you react if a baby arrived unplanned?

3 How would you cope if you planned a family and none arrived?

4 What problems could either cause between you?

5 The old Prayer Book marriage service particularly emphasizes that the purpose of marriage is to have children. Do you think having children is a necessary ingredient of Christian marriage?

Happy parenting

Good parents need plenty of qualities *and* assets. How would you rate the following in importance?

—Time
—Patience
—Love
—Discipline
—Suitable accommodation
—Faith in God to hand on
—Good health

—Money
—Back-up by grandparents/ neighbours/friends
—Understanding of child-care
—Sense of humour

Waiting in vain

First thoughts of how to prevent a baby's arrival before you are ready to welcome it can change in time to growing disappointment and pain if a wife fails to conceive. Television documentaries have graphically depicted the hurt caused to childless couples and the incredible lengths to which some will go in order to have a child that is their own by birth.

If at some future time you face the problem of infertility (as at least one in ten couples do) you will need to think very carefully and perhaps receive counselling before embarking on the long and sometimes fruitless endeavour to conceive a child. Adoption is no longer an easily achieved alternative. Safer contraceptive methods, an increase in abortion and the likelihood of an unmarried mother keeping her baby, means that there are very few healthy blue-eyed babies to adopt. Many couples instead consider long term fostering, or adopting an older child, or one with handicap or special needs.

7. Preparation for the Church Service

The first person to consult about wedding-day arrangements for a church wedding is the minister of the church where you wish to be married. He should be given as much notice as possible of the date and time you would like, although your ideas should not be too hard and fast until you have checked with him. At some churches you may need to give as much as twelve months' notice for a Saturday wedding in the popular months of June,

July and August. Six weeks is the absolute minimum for any time of year. Remember that some
clergy are unwilling to marry couples during Lent
(the six weeks before Easter) or Advent (the four
weeks up to Christmas). Others allow weddings at
these times but not flowers in the church.

Talking it over

At your first meeting the minister will book the date
and time and take down other necessary particulars
about you both. Any other marriage preparation you
receive will vary from church to church. It may
include any of the following:

- further interview with
minister, to go over
service, talk about choice
of music and so on
- series of interviews to
deal more widely with the
issues of Christian
marriage
- discussion groups about
marriage with other
engaged couples, led
by trained people
- away courses for
engaged couples in the
diocese
- final pre-wedding
'rehearsal' in church with
the minister

When you marry in church you do so by courtesy of
the minister in charge, so remember to *ask* rather
than tell him what you want! In the Church of
England you must ask the vicar/rector's permission
for:

- the form of service to be
used (Prayer Book or
Alternative Service Book)
- flowers—what colours
and who arranges them
- guest organist
- use of camera/video
camera/tape recording in
church
- use of confetti in church
grounds

Inquire about bells, choir and church organist, as these too have to be booked in advance.

Before the knot is tied . . .

Church of England

Banns must be read in parish church of both bride and groom for three Sundays before wedding (usually three consecutive Sundays) and are effective for three months. This is a public announcement that the two wish to marry and gives an opportunity for anyone who knows a reason why the couple shouldn't marry to say to.

Nonconformist

Visit to Superintendent Registrar to apply for certificate he issues.

1 If you live in different towns, each of you must see the Registrar of your own district.

2 At least twenty-one days' notice is needed. Certificate is valid for next three months.

3 You must each have been living in your normal district(s) for the seven days before you apply.

4 If you are under eighteen, the Registrar will want written proof of your parents' consent.

5 In some churches, the Registrar has to be present at ceremony to hear declarations required by law. Give him/her enough notice of your wedding date.

Other cases

1 If you are a member (and on the electoral roll) of a different church, banns must be read there as well as in your parish church.

2 If one of you is a Roman Catholic and you plan a Church of England wedding, banns must also be read in the parish church where the RC partner lives.

Special arrangements

Church of England

Instead of having banns called you can be married by Common Licence. Apply to the Surrogate (ask parish priest who he is) but one of you must have been living in the parish for at least fifteen days before application.

Archbishop of Canterbury's Special Licence usually only issued in emergencies. Apply to: The Registrar of the Faculty Office, 1 The Sanctuary, London SW1.

To be married by Common or Special Licence, at least one of the couple must be baptized.

Nonconformist

Possible to be married by Superintendent's Licence:
1 Only one of you need apply.
2 He/she must have been living in the district for fifteen days before application.
3 Certificate will be issued one clear day later (not counting Sundays, Christmas Day, Good Friday).

Costs

It is difficult to give exact costs for such items as the publication of banns, the marriage certificate or the Archbishop's Licence, as these vary from year to year. A copy of the statutory fees relating to church weddings can be obtained from The Church Commissioners, Millbank, London SW1.

Your vicar will also be able to let you have these costs, together with any local charges that apply. These will vary with church and district. Some parish churches charge an overall amount for all these administrative costs, which includes a fee to cover the choir, organist, bell-ringing, heating, lighting and cleaning as appropriate.

For a non-church wedding, you will need to contact your local Register Office to find out the costs for a Superintendent Registrar's Certificate or Licence.

Scotland and Ireland

The information given so far applies to couples living in England and Wales. If you live in Scotland, both must complete a marriage notice and take it to the Registrar of the district where you will marry. A week before the wedding, one of you must collect the Marriage Schedule, to be signed after the wedding. For more information write to the Registrar General in Edinburgh. Those in Ireland, contact the Registrar General in Belfast (for Northern Ireland) or Dublin (for Eire).

THE WEDDING

Theme and variations

Some parts of the wedding service will be the same whatever church you get married in, but there are endless variations in order and pattern even in churches of the same denomination. Here are the main ingredients of almost every wedding service:

- prayers—of worship to God and to ask his blessing on the marriage
- hymns and psalms
- address/sermon (sometimes omitted)
- vows—promises made by the couple

- legal requirements— other promises that make the marriage legal
- actions—giving of ring(s) and holding of hands during vows—signing of register

The ceremony is important because:

- God is asked to be present to witness the promises made
- friends, family and congregation are present to witness vows
- God's blessing is asked and God's ideals for marriage are acknowledged

- the legal requirements are observed
- bride and groom publicly witness their belief in Christian marriage and publicly pledge their love and faithfulness to each other

Nonconformist churches

Most of the Nonconformist churches follow a similar pattern to one another. The actual wording and the order of service may be slightly different, but the contents are very much the same.

Roman Catholic Church

Roman Catholics believe that marriage is one of the seven sacraments of their church and the marriage service is combined with the celebration of Nuptial (marriage) Mass. (When one of the couple is not a Roman Catholic it may be decided to have the Marriage Rite without Mass.) So the service begins with prayers and confession and absolution and the marriage ceremony itself is woven into the service for Mass. The priest explains the meaning and purpose of marriage and the usual vows and declarations are made by bridegroom and bride. After the priest has declared them man and wife and the ring or rings have been given, the liturgy of the Mass follows, then the Nuptial Blessing and Communion itself, when the couple themselves may receive both the bread and the wine.

The Society of Friends

For over two hundred years the Friends have had their own distinctive form of marriage service and their own local Registering Officer, who is allowed by law to witness the marriage and the signing of the certificate. The service is always part of the normal Worship Meeting. This is a time of silence when someone or other may give a spoken message. At the beginning, a Friend will explain what a Quaker wedding is like, then the meeting will proceed. Fairly early on the couple themselves will stand up, join hands and declare in turn, 'Friends, I take this my friend (name) to be my wife/husband, promising, through divine assistance, to be unto her/him a loving and faithful husband/wife, so long as we both on earth shall live.' (The wording may vary a little.) They both then sign a certificate of marriage, two more witnesses sign and then the certificate is read aloud by the Registering Officer. Rings may be exchanged, but they are not a part of the actual ceremony. Then the meeting continues with silence, prayers and perhaps a message for the couple.

THE CHURCH SERVICE

In the United Kingdom, as in other countries, marriage is a legal contract and promises must be exchanged in the presence of witnesses and a properly registered person. At a Register Office marriage the contract is signed and sealed before the District Superintendent Registrar. Two statements, required by law, are made at every wedding ceremony and are a part of every church wedding service:

1 I do solemnly declare that I know not of any lawful impediment why I (full names) may not be joined in matrimony to (full names).

2 I call upon these persons here present to witness that I (full names) do take thee (full names) to be my lawful wedded husband/wife.

After they have signed the register, the couple are given their marriage lines, stating that they are man and wife according to the laws of the land.

When you marry in church you are combining the required legal ceremony with a Christian service and Christian vows. Because the Church of England is the state church, all clergy are automatically recognized as registered to perform marriages. In Roman Catholic or nonconformist churches the Registrar must be present unless a minister has been specially authorized and registered to marry. The church building must also be registered for marriages.

The Church of England

Since the Church of England is most commonly chosen for church weddings in Britain, it may help to go over the Anglican marriage service in some detail. Although many people call themselves 'C of E' it can be daunting for them to anticipate the wedding if they are not regular churchgoers. Remember that the minister will give reassurance and help at the pre-wedding 'rehearsal' at the church.

The service itself may be taken from the Prayer book, which was put together over three hundred years ago. The language is very beautiful but very different from today's English. Many Anglican churches now use instead the form of marriage service in the Alternative Service Book (ASB) which is in more contemporary English and introduces the purposes of marriage in a way more suited to present understanding. The familiar promises, however, are unchanged in this version, and appear in almost the same words as the 1662 version, which in turn goes back hundreds of years further still, probably predating the Norman Conquest of 1066.

Both the Prayer Book and the ASB begin by reminding everyone present that:

● marriage was given to men and women by God
● Jesus identified himself with marriage by being a guest at a wedding and making the occasion happy by turning water into wine
● marriage is a picture of Christ's love for his people, the church.

The purposes of marriage are then described, in this order:

PRAYER BOOK
To have children
To avoid immorality
To give each other companionship
For 'mutual society', i.e. help and comfort

ALTERNATIVE SERVICE BOOK
To comfort and help each other
To live faithfully together, come what may
For the enjoyment and benefit of full sexual union
To have children and bring them up in God's ways

Making the promises

The bridegroom and bride are next called upon to make their vows. There are four main parts to this exchange of promises (the ASB wording is in brackets):

1 Any impediment (lawful reason) If there is any legal reason, known by any in the congregation and by either of the two, why the marriage should not take place, it must be stated at this point.

2 Wilt thou have? (Will you take?) Both are asked, in turn, if they will take each other and:

- love
- comfort
- honour (protect)
- keep in sickness and health
- keep only unto him/her (be faithful to him/her) for life

Both in turn answer 'I will'. (The promise to obey and serve, included in the bride's vows in the 1662 Prayer Book, is often omitted when the words of the 1928 revision are used.)

3 I Take Thee (I take you) The minister takes the right hand of bride and groom and joins them. In turn they promise:

- to have and to hold from this day forward
- for better for worse
- for richer for poorer
- in sickness and in health
- to love and to cherish
- till death us do part
- according to God's holy ordinance (law)

4 Putting on the Ring(s) The bridegroom puts the ring on the bride's finger, promising to share himself and all that he has with her. The bride makes a similar promise, whether or not she gives a ring.

The minister then declares the couple husband and wife, saying: 'Those whom God hath joined let no man put asunder' ('That which God has joined let not man divide).

At some point—often at the end of the service—the register is signed by bride and groom, the minister and one parent from each family. There may also be a sermon as well as prayers and Scripture readings and sometimes the couple take Holy Communion together for the first time as husband and wife.

Breaking with tradition

Some couples—or their parents—want the wedding to be completely traditional. Others would like the service to carry their own individual stamp. In some nonconformist churches (Baptist, Methodist and independent churches of various kinds) it may be possible to ask for some change in wording, provided the legally required statements remain intact. You can also 'personalize' the service by:

- choice of music for entering and leaving the church
- musical or other item chosen for congregation while the register is signed

- choice of hymns
- choice of additional/ alternative prayers
- inclusion of a second person to share the taking of the service

You will need to consult the minister and the organist about such choices. Remember, too, to consider the feelings of your guests.

Special cases

Today far more people are concerned about their

Christian commitment than about what particular section of the church they belong to. There are many places where churches of different denominations share services. In some areas Anglicans, Methodists, Baptists and United Reform churches have joined forces completely to form one ecumenical church.

So if the two partners belong to different denominations there should not be the problem there once might have been. The bride's church will probably be the one chosen for the wedding and ministers from both churches may take part in the service. But it is important for a couple to sort out beforehand where they will attend church once they are married. Worshipping God together and belonging to the same church is a great help and strength in marriage.

Belonging to two church families

If one partner is a Roman Catholic, your marriage will be referred to as a 'mixed marriage'. Even though the two people most concerned may have thought out the implications of this, they may find that parents bring pressure to bear because they are unhappy about any child of theirs marrying a Catholic/non-Catholic. Roman Catholic authority discourages such a marriage (for which a special dispensation is necessary) because of problems of worship and the risk to unity of family life.

They ask the Catholic partner to promise not to put his own faith at risk; to endeavour to pass on his faith to children of the marriage; and to respect the partner's faith.

The marriage will usually take place in a Catholic church but permission can be given to be married in another church and may even be encouraged when the bride is the non-Catholic partner. In theory the Catholic priest would be willing to take the service in the Protestant church, but that is not usually acceptable in the Church of England.

The Roman Catholic priest also insists on giving the engaged couple instruction—at least four sessions—and he will encourage them to think through the problems that may arise and to decide what they will do about baptizing their children. All concerned would agree that such couples need to be:

- completely at one in their commitment to Jesus Christ
- able to read the Bible and pray together
- sensitive to each other's beliefs and reactions
- aware of the areas of possible difficulty and be able to talk and pray about them together
- at one in dealing with objections raised by their families

Interchurch Families is an association set up especially to help families where husband and wife have different church allegiances, more often than not a Roman Catholic and a member of another communion. Presidents of the association include the Archbishop of Canterbury, the Cardinal Archbishop of Westminster and the Moderator of the Free Church Council. Write for details and their booklet *Two Church Families* to the secretary: Mrs R. Reardon, The Old Bakery, Danehill, Sussex RH17 7ET; or telephone 0825 790296.

One thing that all Christian churches would agree on—divorce is a last resort and remarriage is only recognized or approved in certain cases. There is likely to be much heartache and searching of conscience by Christians who divorce and wish to remarry. The church tries hard to keep to God's high ideals for marriage but also to show love and understanding to those whose marriages have broken down.

Divorce	Remarriage
●STATE Granted on irretrievable breakdown of marriage.	Legally acceptable.
●ROMAN CATHOLIC Divorce not recognized, since church makes marriages. Church court sometimes grants decree of nullity.	Remarriage of divorcees ruled out, as church regards couple as married to original partners. Only allowed if church court has granted nullity or dissolution.
●PROTESTANT Divorce regarded as last resort. Viewpoints differ among churches. Legal divorce recognized.	No church courts. Each case considered according to church's guide-lines and minister's conscience.
●CHURCH OF ENGLAND Divorce regarded as last resort.	The church is against remarriage when the original partner is still living, although clergy have the right under civil law to take the service, in consultation with the local bishop. A Register Office marriage may be followed by a service of prayer and dedication.

8. Final Countdown and the Day Itself

After the first flurry of activity months beforehand, there may be a time of comparative calm when you can just 'tick over' with the jobs to be done. Once replies to the wedding invitations have been received, you can prepare a seating plan for guests at the reception. It is important to give careful thought to which guests you place together. People want to enjoy themselves at a wedding and much

depends on being in congenial company—whether those who sit together have met before or not. Use all your ingenuity and imagination to match those you place next to one another or at the same small table. If it is only possible to have a standing buffet, do make sure that elderly guests or those with any disability have chairs provided and someone detailed to look after them in an unobtrusive way.

The top table is nearly always set out formally and seating may be arranged like this:

Top table seating plan

Bridesmaid
Bridesmaid
Groom's mother
Bride's father
Bride
Groom
Bride's mother
Groom's father
Chief bridesmaid
Best man

Tone indicates groom and his relatives and friends

An alternative order is: Best Man, Bridegroom's Mother, Bride's Father, Bride, Bridegroom, Bride's Mother, Bridegroom's Father, Chief Bridesmaid.

You have done all you can in advance—but ahead there looms the prospect of those frantic last weeks and days before the wedding day itself. Many of the last-minute jobs just cannot be done earlier. But at least you can keep well up to date and on top of things—and quell rising panic by making lists and yet more lists that will stand you in good stead when you are caught up in the rising excitement and calm thinking is more difficult. Here are some lists which may help.

WHO DOES WHAT?

These are the duties of the main persons involved. Give a copy to each as appropriate.

Best man

- keep in touch with the bride's family beforehand about all arrangements
- see that the bridegroom's going-away clothes are at the hotel/reception hall
- see that the ushers' buttonholes and service sheets are at the church
- look after the bridegroom—take him/accompany him to church, sit beside him
- make sure the bridegroom pays necessary fees at church, or hand them over for him before/after service; give him moral support
- look after the ring and hand it to the minister at the right moment in the service
- oversee the ushers after the service
- make sure all guests are into cars before leaving yourself for the reception
- act as master of ceremonies at the reception (unless hotel provides MC)
- announce speeches and cutting of the cake, and read out selected greetings/cards
- reply to the toast to the bridesmaids

● announce when the bridal couple are leaving for the honeymoon and organize travel to the airport/station when necessary

● take charge of the bridegroom's wedding suit and return to the house/hire company

Ushers

● arrive at church at least forty minutes before the service is due to begin
● hand service sheets to guests and conduct them to prearranged or suitable pew (bride's guests on the left and bridegroom's on the right, with close relatives/friends nearer the front)
● escort bride's mother to her place (reserve a space beside her for the bride's father, who will join her part-way through the service)
● organize lifts to the reception for guests, under the best man's supervision.
(If maps were not included with invitations, ushers should have maps or clear instructions for the route to the reception and parking facilities there.)

Chief bridesmaid

● help the bride to dress on the wedding day
● look after small attendants
● take the bride's bouquet before the service begins
● return the bouquet after the service (probably in the vestry after the signing of the register)
● help the bride to change after the reception and look after her wedding clothes afterwards

Bride's father

● take care of the bride when everyone else has left for church
● travel to church in the car with her
● pose with her for photographers before entering the church
● lead her up the aisle, on your right arm
● stand beside the bride. The minister will

instruct on how to respond
● sit in the seat reserved beside your wife

● greet guests, as host, at the reception
● propose the toast of bride and groom

Now make a list of all the outstanding duties of the last few days which may include:

COLLECT:
● wedding cake
● cake stand and knife
● flowers for arranging in church and at reception
● hire clothes
● foreign currency
● service sheets

TAKE:
● announcement form to local paper
● place names, special napkins, etc. to hall/hotel
● service sheets to best man or direct to church
● going away clothes and honeymoon luggage to hotel
● final numbers to hotel/ caterers

Don't forget to arrange for all main participants to be at church for pre-wedding run-through.

Helping hands

Kind friends and neighbours may offer help. Be ready with some practical suggestions, if they are in earnest. For example, they could:

● arrange flowers at church/reception
● give lifts to church/reception or meet guests at station/airport
● do last-minute ironing
● provide overnight accommodation for long-distance guests
● offer coffee and wash-and-brush-up facilities to on-the-day arrivals from a distance
● do last-minute

preparation/presentation of food if you do your own catering
● some 'angel' who is not a guest might even tidy up the house ready for the return of friends after the wedding

---

THE DAY ITSELF

Ideally all the previous preparation should mean that the bride is free to get ready without fuss and rush. Make sure that there are enough willing helpers on hand to deal with any last-minute crises.

Final countdown

● **Zero minus forty minutes:**   ushers arrive at church

● **Zero minus thirty minutes:**   best man and groom arrive at church

● **Zero minus twenty-five minutes:**   guests begin to arrive

● **Zero minus ten minutes:**   bride's mother and bridesmaids arrive; bridesmaids wait in the porch (some say bride's mother should be last to take her seat, just before arrival of bride).

● **Zero minus five minutes:**	bride and father arrive (this allows time for photographs and arranging dress/train before procession up aisle)
● **Zero:**	usher gives prearranged signal to organist; organ plays; bride and her father walk slowly up aisle

Timing

Weddings always take more time than expected. The service may be brief—say thirty to forty minutes—but photographs, transport of all guests to the reception and preliminaries once there all take time, and that is before the meal is eaten, the cake is cut, or the speeches made. The distance from the church to the reception will affect the timing, but allow a good two to two-and-a-half hours from the start of the service to the beginning of the meal.

The reception

Bride and bridegroom are the first to leave the church, followed by both sets of parents and the attendants. They should arrive in time to greet guests in a receiving line in this order:

1 bride's parents   **3** bride and bridegroom
2 bridegroom's parents   **4** attendants

This may seem formal but it does give both families the chance to meet all the guests, and guests the opportunity to thank their host and hostess and congratulate the happy couple. Guests should not stay chatting but move quickly down the line, leaving time and space for others. They can then circulate among other guests clutching their fruit juice or sherry.

Programme of events

Here is a suggested sequence of events during the reception:

1 grace before the meal, said by minister or chosen relative/friend

2 meal

3 speech from bride's father: he will propose toast to bride and bridegroom

4 reply from bridegroom who proposes toast to bridesmaid(s)

5 best man's reply to toast

6 best man reads suitable selection of greetings cards/ telemessages

7 bride and bridegroom cut cake

8 bride and bridegroom go to each table to talk to all guests

9 bride and bridegroom leave to change, returning in going-away clothes

10 best man announces departure of couple

11 guests see the couple off

There are many possible variations for the end of the programme, depending on whether there is a disco, a further reception at the bride's house, or an evening dance/party to follow.

Making speeches

Some bridegrooms and fathers of the bride shake in their shoes at the thought of making a speech. *Don't* send away for an advertised readymade speech— that's just what it will sound like. Instead:

● think out and jot down the main points you wish to cover

● keep it brief

● talk naturally, as if to one or two good friends in your own living-room

● avoid stories that could

- embarrass the bride or bridegroom
- don't be too rude or too fulsome in praise of your daughter (bride's father)
- avoid blue jokes: they are not appreciated by everyone
- don't read your speech word for word
- if you are afraid of drying up or fading out, write out a good, punchy closing sentence to end your short, crisp speech, and read it out

Bridegroom: the main purpose of *your* speech is to thank everyone, including:

- the bride's parents (for her and for the reception)
- guests (for coming and for presents)
- your parents (for all they have done for you)
- bridesmaids (for being beautiful as well as useful)

Finish by proposing a toast to the bridesmaids.

After it's all over

Don't forget to arrange ahead of time for someone to collect and take away:

- the bride's and bridegroom's wedding outfits
- flowers
- wedding cake (stand/knife if hired from elsewhere)

The bride will have disposed of her own bouquet according to her fancy.

9. The Honeymoon

To judge from the advertisement pages of some glossy magazines, it would seem that most couples jet off to some exotic spot for a romantic honeymoon the moment the wedding is over. If you can afford this kind of holiday of a lifetime, and feel that the honeymoon is the best time to have it, you may well go ahead with such plans. But before assuming that in order to do everything 'properly' you must follow up an expensive wedding with an expensive honeymoon, take a long hard look at what you really *want* and what you can reasonably *afford*.

WHAT DO YOU THINK?

1 You will have spent months planning a complicated operation—your wedding. Can you spare time and energy to plan a holiday successfully at the same time?
2 You are already spending a great deal of money and have many expenses ahead. Can you afford a luxury holiday too?
3 Will you feel like a long journey and totally different environment after the tiring events of the run-up to the day and the day itself?

If the answer is 'yes' in every case, you will be going to Bali or the Bahamas from choice and not because of sales pressure. But you may prefer to spend much of the time off work getting settled into your new home, or relaxing at some quiet spot in this country.

Alternative suggestions
● a few days to recover from the excitement and exhaustion before flying off to a holiday abroad
● a short break (Paris/Amsterdam) before returning to the new home

Making plans

Book well ahead for a honeymoon holiday, especially if your wedding is at a popular holiday time. Go to a reputable travel agent. If you want a honeymoon package ask for firms who provide them, with a bridal suite, champagne and flowers. In fact, if you indicate on your booking form that you are a honeymoon couple, special extras will be included anyway.

For a holiday in the United Kingdom contact the British Travel Centre, 12 Regent Street, London SW1Y 4PQ (telephone 01-730 3400) for advice.

Tourist Information Services supply addresses for accommodation (your local Tourist Information Centre—see the telephone directory—will provide address for the town/area of your choice).

Holiday preparation

Passport If the bride wants a passport changed to her married name she should fill in the appropriate form from the Post Office and send it off six weeks before it is needed. It must also be signed by the minister who will marry her. The new passport will be postdated to the wedding. Alternatively she may use her existing passport and take her marriage lines with her to show that she is married and travelling with her husband.

Money Eurocheques can be used on the continent but some loose change in local currency will also be needed. Travellers' cheques are still probably the safest form of money to carry around. Your travel agent and bank will advise you. Remember that banks close at 3.30 p.m. Collect currency in good time on Friday for a Saturday wedding.

Clothes Put clothes for the holiday in a separate place. Pack and label cases in good time.

Inoculations Travel information will include advice on any jabs necessary for your destination. Doctors' surgeries also keep a list, issued monthly by the Ministry of Health, showing the protection recommended for every country. Get what you need well in advance of wedding busyness.

Opinion seems to be divided between those who remember their honeymoon as a cloud nine experience and others who admit that it was more or less of a disaster. For most it is probably a mixture of ecstasy and exasperation. Couples coming together and beginning to live together for the first time are bound to find that there are a great many adjustments to be made. Remember that:

- you are tired from months of exhausting planning and anticipation
- the big day took it out of you in sheer physical and emotional effort
- being together every minute of every day and every night is exciting but also demanding, especially for those used to time and space of their own
- love-making does not always go right for both the first time, all the time, or every time.
- you bring to marriage different lifestyles, different daily habits and different expectations.

You may have quite distinct and definite views on small things which can yet loom large. Do you sleep with the window open? Do you read in bed? Do you drink early morning tea? Do you chatter the moment you wake or stay silent until breakfast is over? And that is just the beginning!

Making love

We have commented already on the stand many Christians are making these days about the way sex instincts are being exploited for hard cash. They are sometimes accused of implying that sex is not quite nice, when they are really saying that sex is far too good and important to be misused and squandered.

Some people picture God as an almighty policeman, ready to pounce the moment he catches us enjoying ourselves. The truth is quite the opposite. In the New Testament we are told that every good gift comes from God. Sex is one of God's very special gifts to us. God gave sex as the way to carry on the human race but he intended it to be much more. It is intensely pleasure-giving and is the perfect way for a husband and wife to express their love for each other. The sex act joins the whole of us—not just our bodies—together and makes two people completely one.

On the first night together after the wedding and the journey, both partners will be feeling tired, so for some couples initial love-making should be gentle and patient rather than demanding. Remember that as husband and wife:

- you have all the time in the world to get to know each other's body and each other's responses
- there is none of the strain and stress of a 'one night stand' or a trial relationship, demanding that you get it right first time

- because you love each other and have promised to cherish and comfort each other, you aim to give as well as take pleasure
- this is only the beginning of a physical love that will enrich you and satisfy you for the rest of your lives together

Plenty of books are available on how to gain maximum satisfaction from making love. Such manuals can be helpful but it is important to realize that making love is much more than mastering a technique correctly. A lot of couples may be concentrating on getting it right when what really matters is using sex to share your mutual love in the ways that give pleasure to you both and bring satisfaction and fulfilment. There are no fixed rules as to how often or in what ways you make love, except that each will consider the other's feelings in this as in other matters.

In your continuing physical relationship shared sex will develop and grow in depth and enjoyment. Remember that:

- making love should be spontaneous—not always in the same way, at the same time, or in the same place

- making love can be passionate and intense—it can also be fun!
- making love should satisfy both husband and wife

10. Setting up Home

When you are married you will want a place of your own if it is at all possible. One of you may already have a flat or house where you can live—at least for a start. Or you may need to rent or buy property together straight away. There are advantages in buying.

Buying
- payments are making the house yours
- repayments may be less than rent
- there is tax relief on mortgage loan repayments
- you can decorate and improve your own property

Renting
- unfurnished property is scarce
- rented property is expensive
- sometimes difficult to get urgent repairs done

Renting

The safest type of house to rent is council property. Provided you are eighteen years of age, and subject to certain residential qualifications, you may register on your local council's waiting list. A points' system normally gives preference to those with greatest housing needs. An engaged couple may register but will not be considered for an offer until the date of their marriage.

Buying

The prospect of buying a flat/maisonette/house is daunting. There is so much mystique about the whole business and the sums involved are so much higher than for any other purchase you make. Here are the steps to be taken:

1 Approach a building society or bank to see how much money they would be prepared to lend you. When money to lend is scarce, building societies give preference to those who already save with them. In the case of a bank it is convenient to borrow from the bank you normally use.

Building Society loan
A Building Society will lend you roughly two-and-a-half times the gross annual income of the higher earner (man or woman) plus the amount of the other income.

Bank loan
The amount is based on a formula of three times the gross income of the higher earner or twice the joint income. (NB Overtime is not taken into account.)

2 Look for property within the price range dictated by the amount you can borrow. Remember that over and above the cost of the house you will need enough money to pay for:

- the difference between the loan and the actual cost of the house (Most building societies/banks offer 80% or more of **their** valuation of the property, which is often lower than the asking price. If you **do** get the house for less than their valuation they will only lend on the basis of that lower sum.)

- house valuation and survey
- land registry fee
- conveyancing fees
- stamp duty on property over £30,000
- repairs/improvements which may be a condition of the loan, laid down by the building society
- any decorating you wish to do, plus furnishing, etc.

3 Make an offer, subject to 'survey and contract'. (NB in Scotland procedure is different—see recommended booklet.)

4 Return to the building society or bank to ask for a definite loan.

5 Arrange a structural survey (especially necessary in the case of an older house). Ask the building society if they will combine their valuation with a more detailed report for your use. This will save expense. Or the society may offer you a report that costs less than a structural survey but tells you more than a basic valuation would.

6 Find a conveyancer. Solicitors no longer have the monopoly and, because of competition, are readier to offer a reasonable package deal. Don't mind asking around. Do-it-yourself conveyancing saves money but can be risky. If you overlook the fact that a motorway is due to run through the living-room of your dream house you could be paying out far more than conveyancer's fees.

7 Contracts are exchanged once local searches have been made and other inquiries carried out to make sure that there is nothing to your disadvantage about the land or the property. At this stage 10 per cent of the purchase price is paid to the solicitor who holds it for the owner. The contract is now binding.

8 Completion takes place about a month later. The rest of the money is paid via solicitors, and the house is all yours.

Insurance

Most building societies and banks who lend money for a property will insist on your taking out a life assurance policy to cover the loan. Take it out on a joint life basis, so that the sum assured covers both husband and wife should either die during the term of the loan. If you have a *capital repayment* mortgage then take out a mortgage protection policy with the insurance company. This policy would pay off the remaining sum owed on the mortgage should one of you die. An alternative method of financing a mortgage (often more attractive to young couples) is to take out a *low cost endowment policy*.

Instead of paying off the sum of the capital owed to the building society or bank the borrower pays only the interest due each month. Premiums are also paid to an endowment insurance policy under which a capital sum is built up. If one of the couple dies during the term of the loan, the policy pays off the amount borrowed. If both are still living when the mortgage term ends, the policy pays out a cash sum, normally enough to pay off the loan with some cash left over.

Remember that you *must* insure property—against fire and other risks—for its full replacement value. House contents should be insured (enough to buy *new* all that the house contains). Permanent health insurance is also recommended for self-employed people. Additional life assurance is worth considering for both—payments are small.

Government help for first time buyers is worth inquiring into. Ask your building society about it because the government loan is linked to the amount you have saved over at least the last two years and these savings must be kept in a special account.

Books to help

Buying a House or Flat, published by Bedford Square Press
Buying Your Home, free on request from Scottish Widows Fund and Life Assurance Society, 15 Dalkeith Road, Edinburgh EH16 5BU

Building Societies and House Purchase and **Building Societies and House Purchase in Scotland** (where the system is different) obtainable free from The Building Societies Association, 3 Savile Row, London W1X 1AF

HOME IS MORE THAN A HOUSE

Just as marriage is more than a wedding, so a home is more than a house. A good bit had to be said about the practicalities of buying or renting accommodation but making that living space into a home is a far more important matter. The moment we step into someone's house—or even their bedsit—we can sense if it is a real home, though we might find it hard to explain in words what makes the transformation.

Gazing at shop windows, looking at advertisements, or even listening to others talk might lead us to think that matching curtains with carpet, preserving the period of a house, or decorating in perfect taste are what matter most. Deep down we know that is just not true.

When a house ceases to be an object in its own right and supplies the needs of its occupants and reflects their attitudes, it begins to take on the character of a home. Your house will reflect *your* priorities and *your* values. For some particularly sensitive people a house even seems to give out the feelings and experiences of those who have loved or hated, prayed or quarrelled within its walls. Whether you know it or not, the property you acquire from the estate agent's list will soon take on something of your own characters.

WHAT DO YOU THINK?

● Is your home to be an object of beauty enjoyed and cherished for its own sake—or a pleasing background to living, cleaned when the dirt actually shows? Or do you want something between these extremes?

● Do you plan set dinner parties—or prefer to let friends drop in for coffee when you or they feel like it? Or something between?

● Is your home to be a refuge to which you both return whenever you can—or a 'pad' from which to launch into the outside world and go out and about?

● What kind of home would you want to create for your family? What qualities of a home count most for children?

A Christian home

For those who take Christian marriage seriously, God is as important a person in the new home as he was in church on the wedding day. Putting him at the centre of married life means making God's standards (taught in the Bible) the standards of the home.

Jesus said that 'a person's true life is not made up of the things he owns, however rich he may be' (Luke's Gospel 12:15). He also told his followers that real hospitality involves inviting to your home those with special needs who aren't even in a position to invite you back (Luke 14). The New Testament word for hospitality literally means 'love for strangers'. A Christian home which is open to all who need its acceptance, warmth and understanding comfort will reflect the welcoming love of God.

A Christian home is also one where Jesus Christ is present and is obeyed. Anger, argument and misery may appear, but need be temporary residents only. Christ's forgiveness, peace and joy can transform the home as well as those who live in it. This can happen without the owners even knowing—but the visitors will notice.

In a Christian home the Bible is read and those who live there pray together often. They share together in the family life of the church.

ONE OF THE FAMILY

It's a time-honoured custom for the bride's father to refer, in his wedding speech, to 'gaining a son, not losing a daughter'. Marriage certainly brings the enrichment of belonging to a second family. But age-old mother-in-law jokes imply that an additional set of parents is not always an unqualified blessing.

Most parents want the best for their son or daughter. But it isn't easy—perhaps particularly for mothers—to take second place in the affections of the child they have brought up and been closely involved with since babyhood. These days, of course, many parents have made the break years before, when the son or daughter left home to go to university or to look for work. Such parents are often only too thankful that their older 'child' has settled down with a marriage partner.

Whether parents are hostile or approving, from the wedding day onwards the new husband and wife must be clear in their own minds about the place of their respective parents.

The Bible makes the statement that in marriage a man and woman leave mother and father and cleave to each other. What do you think that statement implies? Some, or all, of these conditions?

● that both leave the parental home and set up house together?

● that husband and wife give each other top priority, even above relationships which counted most before marriage?

● that husband and wife make their own decisions without undue influence from parents and families?

● that husband and wife are completely loyal to each other; rows, money worries, employment problems, are not repeated to parents on either side without mutual consent?

● that visits to and from parents must be kept at a level that both husband and wife can agree to?

There is no need to assume that relationships will be tricky. With a little tact and imagination on both sides, husband and wife can be enriched by the increased family circle. But interference and possessiveness call for kind but firm action from the word go.

The other family

A couple who are married in church declare their vows not only in the presence of their own two families but of God's family too. Those who have committed themselves to Jesus Christ are God's children and part of a huge family that worships God and shares life together in churches throughout the world. The church family that has witnessed the marriage vows will be there to give friendship and support to the couple in the years that lie ahead. Wherever they go to live, there will be Christians to welcome them into the local branch of the church family.

11. Managing the Money

Money can be a big headache and a recurring cause of friction in a marriage, so all the more reason to get things sorted out as efficiently as possible. Both partners need to understand what's going on, even if the one who is 'good with money' does the handling of affairs.

1 Assess how much will be coming in each month —probably the sum of your two salaries (after tax, pension contribution and National Insurance deductions).

2 Now list your monthly expenditure. There may be a bit of guesswork at first for such items as fuel bills, but estimate on the high side. Here are some of the items that make up outgoings:

- mortgage or rent
- rates/water rates
- gas, coal, electricity
- insurance
- television/video rental + licence
- telephone
- food
- clothes
- fares, season ticket
- car tax and insurance
- cleaning materials
- toiletries
- gifts (personal/good causes/church)
- subscriptions
- newspapers/magazines
- entertaining
- entertainment
- books/records, etc.

Some of the items you once considered necessary may become luxuries now that you are householders with sizeable payments to make.

3 Keep a check on your expenditure every month to discover just where the money *is* going and see how you can cut back when necessary.

Offers of help

Not all the schemes advertised to solve your money worries help in the long run. Credit cards and store charge cards are useful but can involve high rates of interest (see *very* small print) when repayment is delayed.

Bills which crop up quarterly or annually (e.g. a season ticket) can cause problems. Some banks will arrange so-called budget accounts or revolving credit accounts to provide for these quarterly or annual payments by spreading the cost evenly. The Gas and Electricity Boards and British Telecom have schemes for equal monthly payments based on their estimate of your consumption for the year. They all issue stamps, too, to help you save towards the total cost of the bill when it comes in. The Post Office also sells television stamps towards the licence fee.

But these methods do mean that you are parting with your money in advance. It might be better to open a special building society account and pay money into it towards your bills, so that it can be gaining interest while you wait for the bills to arrive.

Emergency Fund Once you own property you can never be sure when expenses will occur. Keep an emergency fund in a building society account, which you never touch—except in emergency! Then top it up again as soon as possible.

Giving it away

If you wait to see what is left over when all expenses have been met you will find very little to spare for giving to people in need or to the church where you belong. But Christians think it important to put giving to God and to others high on the list of commitments. Such giving is:

- a natural response to God's generosity to us
- a demonstration that all we have and are belongs to God
- a way of saying thank you to God
- a practical response to the needs of others

In Old Testament times the Jews were taught to tithe—give one-tenth of their income to God. Some

Christians feel that this is a fair proportion; others give much more. The New Testament teaches Christians to work hard, not in order to raise their own living standards, but so as to have more to give to those in need.

Tax

Whenever in the year you get married, adjustments will be made to give you the right proportion of the married man's allowance. Report your marriage to the tax office—Form 11PA. There are two different schemes for being taxed separately rather than as a married couple. One of these involves forgoing the married man's allowance. See leaflets IR13, IR31 and IR32, from your local tax office.

Everything in its place

Money matters are far less bother when you know what your financial position is at a glance and can lay your hands on documents at a moment's notice.

Keep a cash book for all your financial transactions and check totals against bank statements.

Use files with dividers to make your own personal filing system. Mark dividers with main subjects— rates, electricity, etc.—and keep all bills in the right compartment.

Keep another file for household, furnishings, car, etc. and clip receipts to guarantees and any other documents that may be needed.

Note the main expenses for every month and list the addresses and phone numbers of the bank, building society, tax office and so on.

When you've sorted out a system that suits you, update it regularly.

Postscript

When you get married you both need to make new wills. This is *not* morbid (and will certainly not hasten death in some mysterious way) but a common-sense and businesslike way to smooth out further difficulties for your partner and family should the unexpected happen. Do it without delay!

12. Marriage that will Last

Every couple *hopes* for a marriage that will last. In a church wedding the bride and bridegroom go further. Each promises to take the other 'from this day forward ... till death us do part, according to God's holy law', and declares that 'this is my solemn vow'. Such a vow may be hard to keep in a society with different attitudes about the permanence of marriage.

Think positive!

We live in an age of built-in obsolescence. We are accustomed to the idea of a washing machine that lasts five years or so, instead of the lifetime our parents expected. At the back of our mind is the knowledge that should the present machine break down it would probably be less trouble and cost to replace it rather than have it repaired.

No one is likely to think of a marriage partner in the same category as a household appliance, but the same philosophy of change permeates our society. Maintaining and renewing an existing marriage *is* costly in terms of time, effort and personal sacrifice.

There is a school of thought that asserts that it is not even desirable to pay such a price. These advisers insist that marriages are likely to wear out and that the liberating and mature way forward is to let them go. If such negative thinking is built into a marriage there is not much chance that it will survive difficulties.

Once a couple accepts at the deepest level of thinking that their marriage is for keeps they will explore every way of keeping it alive and healthy, whatever the cost. Of course, people do change, but with due care and attention couples can grow and change *together* instead of apart.

Keep talking!

Women have the stereotype reputation for chattering ceaselessly to husbands who merely nod or grunt in return. That may not matter too much when it comes to passing on the day's happenings, but there are other areas where one-sided conversations will not be enough.

Women may find it easier to analyse their feelings and their marriage than men do, but real and honest talking on both sides is needed when it comes to issues that concern each personally or both together. In practice it means finding time, opportunity and energy to discuss:

- money worries
- employment worries
- fears about health
- problems about the children/parents
- difficulties at work
- relationship with God
- relationships with friends/colleagues
- relationship together

Listen!

If both are going to talk, both must listen too—and that involves hearing what has *not* been said as well as the words actually spoken. Feelings of dissatisfaction or a cry for help may not be put into words. Listening because you care enough to want to hear means helping the other to confide fully and find relief in doing so.

Vive La Différence!

Some people imply that biological differences are the only ones between men and women. Many men are sensitive and gentle (characteristics we often think of as female) and women may be aggressive and tough (typically male characteristics). But broadly speaking there *are* male and female characteristics not solely biological nor merely the result of conditioning.

In New Testament times the early church taught that a man is the head of his wife and that a wife should submit to that headship. Many people see this as a degrading way to depict the marriage partnership. For us today the word 'head' conjures up an image of an authoritarian figure, like a head-master or head of department, while the word 'submit' gives the impression of timid subservience. One present-day Christian writer, John Stott, corrects this interpretation by explaining that the husband's headship has nothing to do with superiority but defines his role as protector, giving the woman space and confidence to develop the vulnerable female characteristics of gentleness and sensitivity that could be crushed in the rough and tumble of life. The wife's submission refers to her willingness to allow her husband to provide such protection. Both partners are equal and both provide the right environment for their different but complementary qualities to flourish and reach maturity.

Be honest!

Keeping small things back or telling white lies may not seem important but complete frankness in marriage is a solid foundation for a relationship that can endure. In a healthy marriage honesty extends to telling each other the truth about faults or weaknesses. The brutal truth need not be brutally told. The New Testament singles out 'speaking the truth in love' as an important ingredient of growing up together. There *is* a marital tightrope to be walked. Husband and wife depend on each other for fostering their own self-image. Everyone needs a partner who can boost confidence and make him/her feel accepted and lovable. Somehow the truth must be told without damaging the other's ego too badly or harming the relationship.

Regular servicing

Honest assessment of your relationship can be useful from time to time, whether you are just engaged or a long-married couple. Dr Smilkstein devised an index that helps couples discover how far they are meeting each other's needs. He insisted that assessment should be followed by talking over those needs and telling your partner of the problem, rather than by suggesting how you think he/she should solve it.

The Apgar Index

Answers: A: Almost always; B: Some of the time; C: Hardly ever

1 I'm satisfied with the help I receive from my partner when something is troubling me.

2 I'm satisfied with the way my partner discusses items of common interest and shares solving our problems.

3 I find that my partner accepts my wishes to take on new activities or make changes in my lifestyle.

4 I'm satisfied with the way my partner expresses affection and responds to my feelings, such as anger, sorrow and love.

5 I'm satisfied with the way my partner and I share time together.

Scoring: A = 2 B = 1 C = 0

Scores

10–7 Partner is meeting all or almost all emotional needs

6–4 Moderately satisfied

3–0 Deep problems in the relationship

Sex

A survey came up with the fact that many marriages that begin with sex unlimited quite quickly become marriages with little or no sex at all. When this happens many couples are conscious that an important ingredient in the relationship is missing and are specially vulnerable to exciting signals from other members of the opposite sex. Others go along with the theory that sex is not necessary to marriage anyway and is soon outgrown. One such person described sex as a 'tight contained thing within itself' rather than a vital part of the whole marriage. Such thinking may spring from a view of sex as a physical experience only—to be enjoyed with anyone attractive—or as a means of self-gratification.

Sex in a vacuum, used only for personal and immediate pleasure is likely to grow stale even within the context of marriage. But the sex act can also:

- express shared love in a way no words can do
- maintain the close bond between the couple
- be the perfect way of giving the whole self to the other
- create an opportunity to understand and meet the other's needs, as well as gaining personal pleasure and satisfaction

The sex relationship may wither through boredom. Making love in the same way in the same place at the same time can be dreary. A good sexual relationship requires an effort to please as well as to gain pleasure.

Talk about your sex life—try to tell each other about the pleasures and disappointments and find ways of improving and maintaining a satisfying relationship throughout your marriage—however long it may last.

Anger

Sooner or later anger will erupt in your marriage. How you deal with it will differ according to patterns learned from childhood, or to how you think you are expected to react. Many people feel guilty about being angry but anger is a natural human emotion and is not always wrong. It was anger that motivated the great reformers to fight slavery or child prostitution, and anger sparked off the more recent aid programmes to feed the world's hungry.

More often, though, anger *is* wrong because it springs from self-pity, self-interest or hurt pride. Anger may show itself in a raised voice, a red face, and raised fists, but it can also appear in the form of obvious silence and sulking, or withdrawn behaviour. Anger that is neither expressed nor even admitted by the person concerned can lead to depression or physical illness.

It is hard to break the mould of your own pattern of reacting to anger and it may also be difficult to cope with a partner who reacts in a very different way. Somehow you must find a way of talking about and discharging your anger with the least possible harm to the marriage. Trying to pretend it isn't there will store up far worse trouble for you both. Learning to see the funny side and laugh instead of rage is an ideal solution. Calling a truce until you have both calmed down is another way round. However you cope, it is important to remember the Bible's guidelines:

● 'If you become angry, don't let your anger lead you into sin' (beware the snowball effects of anger!)

● 'Don't stay angry all day' also translated 'Never go to bed angry' (make it up quickly!)

These instructions limit the worst and lasting effects of anger.

Saying sorry

Some people find it almost impossible to say sorry. They may show that they want to make it up but they cannot bring themselves to utter the words, 'I'm sorry—I was wrong.' To admit to being wrong and to ask forgiveness calls for maturity, humility and enough confidence to know that the world won't collapse because you've made a mistake.

Forgiveness

Forgiving one another is the other side of the coin. Sometimes marriage partners are called upon to forgive deep wrongs, and forgiveness can seem impossible. Christians are told to be 'kind and tender-hearted to one another', and to 'forgive one another, as God has forgiven you through Christ.' They have good reason to forgive and they have help from God to do so. God's forgiveness and his help in forgiving others are open to all.

What do you think?

1 What practical problems could there be in a marriage—
● for the partner who has to forgive?
● for the partner who has to ask and accept forgiveness?

2 What does each need to do—and not do—if the relationship is to go on growing in mutual love and trust?

Space to be yourself

Endless jokes are made about being tied to a wife or husband. It is only too easy for a possessive partner to make the other feel stifled and cramped. Every person needs the opportunity to develop as an individual and couples will vary in the amount of breathing-space they need. Unemployment or early retirement may mean that a couple spend days as well as nights together. They may need deliberately to plan some time apart in order to keep the marriage healthy. Other couples are kept apart by work all day and some evenings and weekends too.

What do you think about time together?

1 Should you make hard and fast rules about time together and time apart?

2 Should you always . . .

- go to bed at the same time?
- get up at the same time?
- go on holiday together?

- spend weekends together?
- share leisure activities?

Room for God

Many of us are well aware of the guidelines for happy and lasting marriage. But in practice we—and our partners—are too selfish to follow them. The Christian standards for marriage are high but those who commit themselves and their marriage to God have help beyond their own resources. They still face the normal crop of money worries, sickness, loss or unemployment, but they have God to help them. He is at work within the marriage, forgiving and helping them to forgive, able to make something positive from negative experiences and being with them to work out his plans for good, whatever may happen. In such marriages trust in each other is founded on trust in God who never breaks his promises. The possibility of this kind of marriage is open to every couple. God does not have an exclusive arrangement with certain kinds of people only.

'Love is all you need'

Love *is* the key to happy marriage but not just the kind of love that comes naturally. It is love with no strings attached—the kind of love that God offers to us in Jesus Christ. St Paul describes it like this:

> 'Love is patient and kind; love is not jealous, or conceited, or proud; love is not ill-mannered, or selfish, or irritable; love does not keep a record of wrongs; love is not happy with evil, but is happy with the truth. Love never gives up: its faith, hope, and patience never fail. Love is eternal.'
> (From the first letter to the Corinthians, chapter 13, verses 4–8, Good News Bible)

INDEX

NOTES

NOTES

MERE MORALITY

Lewis Smedes

How do we make decisions on the things that matter
most?

Is there a morality for ordinary people?

How can we survive as a humane community?

This very readable, compassionate book has been
written in response to two streams of moral opinion
today: one claims that there are no moral absolutes,
the other that moral life is simple, clear and
unproblematic.

Neither is realistic, says the author. 'I affirm moral
absolutes in the midst of an ambiguous, distorted,
crazy reality. But I also affirm that though these
absolutes give us direction, they do not, in
themselves, give us simplistic answers.'

The focus of the book is the Ten Commandments, in
particular those which call us to respect others. Each
pinpoints the moral nucleus of one sector of life in
community: family, marriage, property,
communication, and the preservation of life itself.

Lewis Smedes is Professor of Theology and the
Philosophy of Religion at Fuller Theological
Seminary, USA.

ISBN 0 85648 546 2

YOUR MARRIAGE
—making it work

Peg and Lee Rankin

How do you choose a life-partner?

How do you set about *living* those marriage vows?

Have you learned to communicate?

Are you determined to stay faithful?

Have you learned to forgive?

Have you worked out your roles and responsibilities?

Do you think 50-50 commitment is enough?

Your Marriage offers practical, down-to-earth help in all these areas and more. It is a book for every couple embarking on marriage who wants to be 'together tomorrow', and for those already married who want their relationship to stay fresh.

Peg and Lee Rankin are experienced team teachers. They have run marriage seminars for many years, and have brought up three sons. Here they share their own experience and that of thousands of other couples in a book which hits hard but is full of laughter. They offer ten consumer-tested principles to build on, and suggest ten commandments for lasting marriage.

ISBN 0 7459 1007 6

COPING WITH DEPRESSION

Myra Chave-Jones

Depression is as universal as the common cold.

It may be little more than a passing mood. It may be a dark shadow, robbing life of all joy. It may make it impossible to carry out the simplest tasks. It may last for only a short time, or drag on for months and years.

What causes depression? How can we recognize it in ourselves and in others? And what help is available?

This is a helpful, practical, sympathetic book for all who suffer from depression, and for those who live close to them.

'A book for which many will be grateful.'
Dr Anne Townsend, *Church of England Newspaper*

'Sensible, sympathetic and positive.'
Church Times

ISBN 0 85648 360 5

WILL MY RABBIT GO TO HEAVEN?

Jeremie Hughes

'Why doesn't the world stop?'
'What happens when you die?'
'Why does God let people do wicked things?'
'How can she have a baby without being married?'

Have you ever been floored by a real poser of a
question from a four-year-old? Or by a genuine
enquiry about some delicate topic from a thoughtful
nine-year-old?

In this book Jeremie Hughes, wife of a Church of
England vicar, journalist and mother of two, has
brought together answers to a wide range of questions
children ask—about death and suffering, about God,
about sex, about heaven and hell . . . It won't give
you *all* the answers. But it may just help you out at
that embarrassing moment when junior pops a
question in the supermarket queue or at Sunday tea
with granny. It may also answer some of the
questions *you've* always wanted to ask . . .

ISBN 0 7459 1221 4

A selection of top titles from LION PUBLISHING

FAMILY/PRACTICAL HELP

COPING WITH DEPRESSION Myra Chave-Jones	£1.50	☐
SINGLE PARENT Maggie Durran	£1.95	☐
THE LONG ROAD HOME Wendy Green	£1.95	☐
FACE TO FACE WITH CANCER Marion Stroud	£3.95	☐
WILL MY RABBIT GO TO HEAVEN?		
Jeremie Hughes	£2.99	☐
SEX AND THAT Michael Lawson/Dr David Skipp	£1.75	☐
ELIZABETH JOY Caroline Philps	£1.50	☐
YOUR MARRIAGE Peg and Lee Rankin	£2.50	☐
FORTY PLUS Mary Batchelor	£3.95	☐
THE STRESS MYTH Richard Ecker	£3.95	☐
MERE MORALITY Lewis Smedes	£1.95	☐
CHARNWOOD Grace Wyatt/Clive Langmead	£2.50	☐

All Lion paperbacks are available from your local bookshop or newsagent, or can be ordered direct from the address below. Just tick the titles you want and fill in the form.

Name (Block Letters) ....

Address ....

....

Write to Lion Publishing, Cash Sales Department, PO Box 11, Falmouth, Cornwall TR10 9EN, England.

Please enclose a cheque or postal order to the value of the cover price plus:

UK: 60p for the first book, 25p for the second book and 15p for each additional book ordered to a maximum charge of £1.90.

OVERSEAS: £1.25 for the first book, 75p for the second book plus 28p per copy for each additional book.

BFPO: 60p for the first book, 25p for the second book plus 15p per copy for the next seven books, thereafter 9p per book.

Lion Publishing reserves the right to show on covers and charge new retail prices which may differ from those previously advertised in the text or elsewhere, and to increase postal rates in accordance with the Post Office.